How to Exi(s)t

How to Exi(s)t

A Poet's Memoir

Truong Tran

CITY LIGHTS BOOKS
SAN FRANCISCO

How to Exi(s)t: A Poet's Memoir

Cover design by Carolyn Ho
Text design by Patrick Barber
Set in DJR Fern Text and MT Neue Kabel

ISBN 978-0-87286-949-3

Library of Congress Cataloging-in-Publication Data

Names: Tran, Truong, 1969– author
Title: How to exi(s)t : a poet's memoir / Truong Tran.
Description: San Francisco : City Lights Books, 2026.
Identifiers: LCCN 2026012592 (print) | LCCN 2026012593 (ebook) | ISBN 9780872869493 paperback | ISBN 9780872869752 ebook
Subjects: LCSH: Tran, Truong, 1969– | Asian American authors | Poets,American | Vietnamese Americans | English teachers—United States | Dyslexics—United States | LCGFT: Autobiographies
Classification: LCC PS3570.R3348 Z46 2026 (print) | LCC PS3570.R3348 (ebook) | DDC 811/.54 [B]—dc23/eng/20260528
LC record available at https://lccn.loc.gov/2026012592
LC ebook record available at https://lccn.loc.gov/2026012593

City Lights Books are published at the City Lights Bookstore
261 Columbus Avenue, San Francisco, CA 94133
citylights.com

Contents

ON BREATHING

ON TEACHING

ON IMAGINATION AND MEMORY

ON FAMILY

ON THE BOOK THAT CAME BEFORE

i am hoarding language. the english language. for a time when this english language. will be revoked. reclaimed. for when i will be told. that writing as i have. is deemed a crime. to write the truth. is to run the hallway. in search of an exit. even so. even when they want you to leave. they wait by the exit. to catch you for leaving.

—*Book of the Other*, page 153

Preface

October 12, 2022. Having just published *Book of the Other: Small in Comparison*, a book about institutional racism and a chronicling of my experiences in academia, I wanted to change fundamentally as a writer. It would have to begin with form. I wrote *Book of the Other* with the consciousness of poetry; I would write *How to Exi(s)t* as stories and essays. *Book of the Other* was the book that I never wanted to write, but it was the book that I had to write. I wrote the book because it happened. I held the consciousness, or more appropriately, the lack of conscience of those who enacted their racism on me. They placed a weight on my shoulders, on my back, and in my pockets that I then carried, this weight of their silence and shame. My life as a writer and teacher has since been a matter of putting that weight down. With *Book of the Other*, I wrote myself out of the unwanted inheritance of that silence and back into existence. I taught myself how to breathe again. By breathe, I am referring to the task of showing up and being present when faced with another's effort of erasure.

If *Book of the Other* was the endeavor of living and enduring, then *How to Exi(s)t* is my assertion of living and thriving. I am doing this by extending the breath of lines into sentences. This book is written as prose and with the newfound freedom of constructed sentences, run-on sentences, and sentence fragments, all existing as they are and who I am. This is a declaration of how I write, with all the complications and imperfections that come with calling myself an immigrant writer of the English language—not a poet but a writer. It is important that I note this distinction, because I spent much of my life defining myself as a poet, only to have a white man come along and casually declare, "He's just a poet." This book, however, is not about the white man, so pardon my digression. Why am I conditioned to ask for forgiveness? I know the answer to this question so I am now asking this of you. Racism has a way of interrupting the moment, a book. This seemingly inadvertent happening has a way of becoming a lifetime.

The sentences used in *How to Exi(s)t* access an inventory of recent and distant narratives. It is in part a concerted practice of dailiness, waking each morning with the desire to say, to put into words the things I've left unsaid for one reason or another. I was busy fighting the latest racist incident. I couldn't get through another book. I was looking for porn. I was falling in love. I was digging in the dirt to hide my family's secrets. I was trying to find my way back home.

All are valid claims for why the narrative of a mother's will to protect her family finds itself in proximity to: the recollection of a boy sitting in a tree witnessing the cruelties of a father exacted on the son. A child's discovery of language and its ties to queerness, erotica, and the self. The struggles of an undiagnosed reality, living with dyslexia as an immigrant child of immigrant parents (that is to say, neither I nor my parents possessed the language to ask for or say what was needed). An encounter with a tenured Ivy League professor in which I was the guest lecturer, giving a talk on the subjectivity of race. I was speaking in someone's house, where again I was a guest, always the guest. Somewhere in all of this was the story of a child who saw fit to take my hands, to give a hug. It was the most honest gift I've ever received.

These are the memories, narratives, and inquiries inside this book. Seemingly disparate yet connected, these threads of thoughts insist on staying knotted and entangled. Their density is the added color to an otherwise white space. Like the conditions of which I speak, the knotted ball of memories, histories, and secrets hidden and exposed, of the things that happened and still happen that make up the sum of who I am. If this reads as something messy and still in process, it's because there's still movement and breathing on my part. It's just another way of saying that I am still confronting the whiteness that is uninvited but ever present as I begin the process of writing every page. These are the essays, stories, and questions that still need asking, arguing, telling, and retelling.

On Writing

On the essay as failed attempt

If the essay is defined as an attempt, then the attempt in this book, as it is with living, should and must at some point or another result in failure. I am not striving towards failure—quite the opposite, in fact. I am trying to write the impossible. Narratives from a place of truth that have been hidden so deep inside the body that they are all but forgotten, except for the persistence of the imagination, the memory that refuses to be written and told as something rendered for consumption, the one statement that needs to be said and yet it hides itself in the obstacle of story after story. I am making a case for these failed attempts at arriving, be it a fragment, a story still without an ending or a succinct argument, to be included in a book of essays and other narratives. What is an attempt if not writing that tries and what is trying if not the acknowledgment of failure? Again, I am writing as though I am asking for permission. This being my book, I give myself permission to try and to fail.

On claiming the stupid

In my daily practice, I write myself into exhaustion at the end of each night. To end on a half-written sentence is to surrender to a language that reminds me of my otherness. This language, with all of its rules of grammar, syntax, and diction, tells me of my place and lack of privilege. I am writing as someone Brown still trying to say, and still failing in all my imperfections, complications, and implications, this claiming of the stupid and the smart and everything in between. I told my former teacher and confidant that I was writing this book, that I was coming out yet again, this time as a writer who struggles with the work of reading a book. He asked if I was certain that I would want to share this with the world, perhaps a warning of the othering still to come. As I am writing this now, I am thinking through his words. I am revising my previous statement. I am writing as someone Brown, writing on the white page.

No. Let's be clear. I am someone Brown writing in a white world, in a white language. I started writing this the night before, and now with clarity and some sleep, I'm still trying to say and still trying to confront, and still failing and still doing it anyway. This is the fundamental change, striving towards and sometimes arriving at some clarity, this breathing that is belabored with uncomfortable truths.

On the strangeness of residency

Part of my praxis is the feeding of others. I want to claim it as a practice for art, that feeding is a metaphor for something bigger, and that there is a need for connecting over food. The act of sitting down together at a table, I want to believe, is the willingness to see one another. I am at a residency where individuals come together to work apart and separate from one another. It is a concept I am still trying to grasp. The awkwardness of strangers cohabitating. We begin each morning as strangers in proximity. We move cautiously through the space, careful not to encroach. The exchange of measured language: How did you sleep? What are you working on today? These are the necessary conditions in the recon of coffee and milk. To venture out only to retreat into isolation is the agenda of each morning. I have been keeping to myself for the most part. I have been writing a lot. I think I'm doing what I'm supposed to be doing. Or is it this? I cook. I make enough to feed the others. I cook as a way of showing myself, of making my presence known. I cook with the effort of considering the other. He doesn't eat meat. She does not eat fish. He is particular but tries not to show it. I drink even though I'm not a drinker. We eat. We talk. We exchange small thoughts that become bigger ideas. And for that hour or two or sometimes even three, we become a world of four, moving in body and in mind as one. We clean the kitchen. We do the dishes. I want to say that this is the art, that this is the work I am supposed to be doing, or is this a condition of being human? I woke up this morning. I wrote these words. I hear the rustling of people making coffee. I hesitate to open my door and step outside into the strangeness of another day.

On editing

Self-censoring is not a practice so much as a condition of existing. I would like to believe that I can say what needs to be said at any given moment, but the reality is there is always a voice in my head telling me to get to the next moment. Sometimes the voice is born of fear and anticipation of being judged by a panel of three white people. The white gaze is made official and decisive, always by a panel of three white people. Other times it is motivated by the need for self-preservation.

Self-censorship implies a choice in the moments or in the lifetime when it happens. This performance of otherness happens because I am conditioned. This is the act of self-preservation. It amounts to cutting yourself down because you get to choose the depth of the cut, the amount of blood you shed in performance. Just to be clear: this is not a performance.

On *I'm angry, goddammit* as contemplation

I made a point to write without anger, as if I could say of anger: *Been there. Done that.* I am ready to move on. I've made this a constraint within my praxis and it has been yielding a bounty of language. In its absence, I've written as a way of looking back. For a minute there, I thought that reflection was my reward for getting beyond this threshold. And then it happened. It happened somewhere in the middle of a sentence. My mother flew and took a bus across a war, two continents, a lifetime's worth of this and that. She got off at this particular stop. The reflection became a wave of regret for all the things I did not do, or say, and all the things I've said, done. Reflection as refraction in a broken mirror. It keeps on breaking, and there in the craze of broken glass, I found my old friend. Hello, anger. I've missed you. I'm here. Can we do this? Together? Can we do both? This looking back. This pushing forward.

On silence, safety, desire, and belonging

It was my last night at the residency. I did not cook. I think my fellow residents were getting tired of my limited flavors. I cook mostly with garlic and onions. My friend taught me rule number one of cooking while broke: all you need is a little garlic, a lot of onions. Everything else is just this and that. Truth be told, I too was getting tired of this and that. This night was also when the partner of a fellow resident would be arriving, a chef and from what I gathered, a legend in the New York food scene. I was intimidated, to say the least. I was in awe before even knowing. She did not disappoint. What little we had left in the cupboards, what bounty was gifted from the garden, was crafted into a delicious dinner. I ate this feast with a sense of gratitude, a knowing of my privilege.

I could end this narrative here. Hold the memory of this transformative time, remind myself that I made new friends, some who I believe will become lifelong friends. When this book comes out, if it comes out, I will give credit to this profound, magical place. This place and its people got me to think, to further my thinking and rethinking. All this would be true but something still has been left unsaid. I have a lifetime of the things I've left unsaid, a mound that has accumulated into a mountain. I am afraid that if I left out this one thing, I would not be able to climb my way over, to get to the other side of knowing. Of knowing the world that I still wanted. If left unsaid, this mountain of things will come crashing down.

It will crater into a chasm. It will keep us separated, divided, apart.

Before the meal, I spoke with Katie, the woman who gardened the land. I barely knew her but still I wanted to be her friend. There was a comfort on the rare occasions when our paths crossed, the chance to acknowledge her presence in this space, to say thank you for the carrots and zucchinis and cucumbers and kale and care. So much care. She told me her story. How she as a Black woman connected with this earth, of the work that comes with tilling the soil and navigating the land, of this need to find and claim her space, of the constant reminders that come with being, being a woman, being Black, being present. The part of living where we have to remind ourselves that we belong. She spoke of wanting safety. This idea of safety as desire left me with a sadness of acute absence. Even as we ate, I learned that her very hands had harvested our bounty. I was filled by the void that comes with my knowledge. I want to say, "I see you, Katie," but who am I kidding? I am the one who wants to be seen. Always wanting to be seen as a way of being present.

Because I did not make that beautiful meal, I did not think it was my place to invite her presence, to ask the question to those who were present, *Why is she not here? Why is she not sitting at this table?* Perhaps she was asked. Perhaps she declined. Perhaps I am asking this of myself to get beyond this condition of my place, knowing this means knowing silence, of my belonging. I laughed along. I ate. I drank. I sat in pockets of silence.

I wrote a lot during my residency. I left early the next morning. I've not really written since that night. I'm trying to write about what happened, about what happens in the absence of language. I'm trying to find the language to hold this memory, to give it purpose. This is me removing the weight that is my foot pressed to my throat. I am invoking Claudia Rankine's image in this instance. I've kept it since reading her words, for when a time came when I needed to see myself relieving myself of this weight pressing down, choking out, silencing a voice already resigned to silence. I'm writing this in the hopes of hearing myself, however low the volume, in the hopes of getting somewhere, getting someplace where we can all belong.

On that shit you can't make up

I will refrain from naming the people and places in this story. Just know that this happened, because it's not possible to make this shit up. After *Book of the Other* was published, I was invited to this Ivy League college to give a series of lectures, readings, and a workshop. I was told by the organizer that I would be speaking in a course titled The Geography of Displacement. I would find commonalities between the book and the class. About three months prior to my visit, I was informed by the organizer of another opportunity; a professor in the English department of this university wanted to invite me to his class to lecture on a particular topic, "Uses of Facts in Creative Writing." It turned out that the professor teaching this particular class was someone I knew. We shared an office at one point.

He was an unnamed participant in my book. When I first received word of his invitation, I panicked. I thought he wanted to confront me for what I wrote. I thought he would do it in front of his class. I wrote an email with the intention of declining the invitation. Somewhere in the course of writing this note, of wanting to break from the conditioned politeness of my being, I said, "Yes." I said, "We know each other." I said, "We go way back." I said he had been kind enough to share an office with a lecturer.

A week prior to arriving at this university, I received another email, this time directly from the professor. He asked that I share some excerpts of my book so that he can share them with his students. It was then that I realized that he had not read the book. Had I shared the excerpts as requested, I don't think that he would have read the book. I decided to send him the book in its entirety, as a digital file, with a note that read, "I cannot do a cut and paste job. It would ruin the integrity of the book's layout and inherent meaning. Here is the book as a pdf and here are the pages you will want to consider." In doing this, I believe this forced him to read the book or, at the very least, the parts of the book that needed to be read by this particular person.

I arrived at the college early on a Tuesday morning. I checked into a hotel and, having accessed my surroundings, I felt the urge to buy a new jacket. I walked the three blocks that made up this town to find that the only men's clothing store was a J.Crew. I refused to wear a J.Crew jacket. I would come as I was, as I am.

My first of a series of lectures took place on a Wednesday morning in the class called The Geography of Displacement. To my surprise, the class was made up entirely of women and taught by a Vietnamese woman. I felt an immediate connection with these students and the teacher. In the middle of my lecture, a young Black woman raised her hand. What she asked I will never forget. "How do you breathe in a place like this?" These might not have been her exact words but this was how I remembered the question. She asked as if she was asking for permission to breathe, to exist, to be. I did not know how to respond, but I have been holding that question ever since that moment when asked. In the same way that I wrote the book that brought me to this story, I am writing this now in hopes that this woman might one day find these words. "You asked as if you were looking for permission. Please know that you should not have to ask for permission. This breathing is your right to claim this space, this being, this breathing. Breathe loud. Breathe proud."

I had coffee with the Vietnamese teacher, who confided in me. She said that her throat felt constricted at the beginning of each day. This process of gaining the will to speak, it was an act of dailiness, of living in this place. She asked about work beyond the academy. We shared a pastry. We exchanged phone numbers. I told her to leave. It was OK to leave. I told her to come for a visit and stay as long as she needed. Stay. These might feel like wanderings from the story but sometimes there are stories inside of stories.

On Wednesday of that week, I received yet another email. I was informed by the organizer that the lecture on "The Uses of Fact in Creative Writing" had to be shortened from its original duration of two hours to an hour in length. The instructor had to do some teaching with his students.

On Thursday, the day of the scheduled lecture, I was informed of yet another amendment to the schedule. The instructor of the class had taken the liberty of sharing my work and that of the organizing professor with his students, in the hopes that we would perform the lecture as a team. I complied. I lectured. I did the work of teaching students. I answered questions launched in my direction and then I answered a question not meant for me. "How do you work with credible facts?" I spoke out of turn. I spoke by asking a question of my own. I don't recall exactly what was said but this is the luxury of telling the story. I get to say what needs to be said.

"How do you work with incredible facts?" For example, I wrote a version of *Book of the Other* 16 years earlier about the discrimination I encountered in the academy. It was called *Four Letter Words*. I wrote it as poetry. I wrote it in a coded language. The discrimination and racism I wrote about, it happened to me and so I wrote about it like I am still writing about it now. But I wrote that first book as a metaphor, because I was afraid. The work of teaching is my life. I define myself first and foremost as a teacher, then a writer, then an artist. I was afraid that, if I was candid, the academy would take away the thing that I loved more than anything else in the world. So I wrote in a language that allowed me to hide inside of language, in metaphor, in plain sight. One could say that I succeeded, having written with this intention. So much so that, on more than one occasion, I was invited into the classrooms of those I wrote about, those who benefited at my expense, to talk about that book, to talk about it in the abstract, to talk about poetry when really there was nothing poetic about discrimination. Metaphor, no matter how hard I tried to find the meaning to being harmed, to being hated, used, and othered, was just a shelter for those who did the work of hating, othering, whiteness.

I saw myself hiding in the metaphorical. I saw the luxury I was affording my inflictors, that they too were hiding inside my metaphors. Or was it the luxury of not having to see? It was there and then, in a classroom not my own, that I made the decision to rewrite *Four Letter Words* as another book. I would tell and retell the story of being discriminated against, of racism. I would write it in no uncertain terms. Still fearful of what they would do, still afraid of losing my livelihood as an adjunct, I wrote *Book of the Other* devoid of names. My agenda was simple the second time around. If I wrote about *you* in *Book of the Other*, if you read it, deliberately or inadvertently, this time around, I wanted to make certain that you will see, that you will *know* that it was about you.

And here I am now, having written *this* book; I am speaking about it in no uncertain terms. For the most part, I've chosen not to use names inside the present book. Perhaps I am still afraid, but I'm not hiding. And the people I'm writing about are still inviting me into their classrooms. These are the facts. You can't make this shit up. How do you work with incredible realities?

The lecture continued in all its awkwardness. In this very public space of a classroom, a very private conversation happened that day. I confronted my inflictor. I got to hear him say he's sorry. Not for what he had done but for the things that had been done by the institution. I got to see his performance of anger. "I'm just so mad that they did this to you." I got to see the wringing of hands. "I left that place before a lot of this happened. I can't imagine how you must feel." I got to witness the rare display of a white man's discomfort in the obligatory lunch that followed the lecture. He ordered his sandwich to go.

That evening, at a reading for the book, I saw this professor sit in the back of the room. I read pre-selected poems, some of which I'd practiced for delivery. I read poems from the many years of my lived experience of being discriminated against. I read one particular poem that spoke of his presence in our sordid history. It was not my intention. I did not think that he would come but he did. I took some time after the reading to sign some books. He bought a copy. He asked me to sign it. I wrote the same thing that I've been writing with each signing:

I hope this book resonates for you.
—Truong

And that was how the story ended.
You can't make this shit up even if you tried.

On translation as loss

I made a statement and was promptly told that I was speaking in hyperbole. This is about translation, so I will take this liberty now. The person who made that remark was a professor, so I could interpret this as academic-speak for: "You don't know what you're talking about. Now shut the fuck up, sit quietly, and listen." That last part is my interjection from a lifetime of being told. It is a translation in a story about translations. The statement in question was simply this: I believe that the modern practice of literary translation is the academy's way of colonizing the other. I should have been more specific. I am talking about white practices in the academy. Before anyone slams this book down on a table or throws it across the room, before someone says, "That's ridiculous" or "Shut the fuck up," let me explain. I have a lifetime of experience in the art of explaining.

I once heard a poem read, once in its native tongue by its writer, and once in another version in English by its translator. The poem, when read in Vietnamese, had a very distinct moment when a tall Black man was described. This read to me as a moment of seeing otherness from the perspective of another. It was to me the essence of the work. When read in English by the American translator, there was no mention of the Black man. Again, I should be more specific here. By "American translator," I am referring to the white translator of the poem. It's quite obvious, I know. But if I didn't say it now, somewhere in the future,

I will be asked to explain myself, as though I would retract my thinking when confronted with the asking.

This glaring omission in that moment felt like a gut punch. And what does one do when one is punched? I punched back instinctively. What I am trying to say here is that sometimes I fight without knowing that I'm fighting. "What happened to the Black man?" I kept my question simple and direct. You might be asking right about now: what does this have to do with colonialism? Wait for it. The translator was clearly taken by surprise. What happened exactly in these transactions between writer and the written, translator and the translated. Did the Vietnamese poet remove the image, having considered his status as an outsider? Is there no room to write about race when writing as the other, as the guest? Did he not want to go there? Did they not go there?

I saw it in the hesitation of the white man's body. He paused in his language and then, as if conjuring fire from his breath, he said, "What Black man?" He said it as though he meant it as a statement, loud and forceful and once again, as a question demanding an explanation. I reiterated my observation that there was a Black man in the Vietnamese version of this poem but somehow not present, perhaps lost, in translation.

Are there casualties in the translation of others? Nothing further was said in that moment, a three-way discourse in the absence of language. What does this have to do with colonialism? Everything. Translation as loss, as surrender, as taking. Translation as the claiming of language, country, and body, as yours. Translation when enacted with little or no effort to understand, with no consideration of belonging. When courses are taught with the use of machines, when partnering with a native speaker to lend credence, to assert a kind of false authority, to validate the work of the translator. Again, I am going to be specific here: I am putting this on the white translator. Call it literature, call it craft, call it an expedition, call it history, call it white colonialism, all over again.

On the essay as an attempt in progress

You skip to the end of a book. You wanted to know and there are still things you want to know. The child is born halfway through the third chapter. Where is he now? Did he grow up to be a good, decent person? His character was kind and caring as a child. You tell yourself he'll be all right. Will he? Did he attend college? Did his mother raise him to be a racist so that he could absorb the racism she anticipated and feared that he would have to endure?

Did the protagonist reconnect with the friend to whom he texted, "You really suck"? Did he ever have that conversation? Did he leave? Did he pack up his belongings, give away his collections of meaningless objects? Did he sell the house? Did he burn it down? What was written in his will? What were his last words?

On sentimentality

The English language has a way of making me want to sound smart. This happens simultaneously with feelings of inadequacy. Does that make sense? This is the dilemma of the constructed sentence when writing is also the act of translating. When really what I want to say is what I see, what I know, what I feel, what I want. "I am hungry. What's for dinner? Eat with me. Be my friend." The other day I said, "I am going to be careful with what I say because I don't want to say something I'll regret." That was more language than what was needed to say, "I love you. I hate you. I don't want to hurt you. I hope these words say what is needed, what I want of myself. What I want of our friendship." Now that I've written this on the page, that's way too much language to say, "Hey, how are you?" The English language has a way of making me feel sappy. At my age, I'll call it sentimental. I'll say that it was earned. I think crying happens in the English language. I'll write those tear-inducing words and then I'll find a way to say I'm sorry for the sentimentality. The literary equivalence was once labeled "confessional" and then the "I word." Oh identity, why must I take this walk of shame? And now just I, the letter I.

On how disparate details make a story

I made my specialty last night to welcome a new friend and her 80-year-old father over for a home-cooked meal. Before telling you of the father, I need to first tell you of the daughter. I've only known her for a little over a month. We met at an artist residency, three thousand miles away, a place supposedly conceived with the intentions of supporting artists and writers, Brown and Black. To our surprise, we were the only presence of color, with the exception of Katie, the gardener.

I think my friend and I will remember this experience for the many complications that it brought to our understanding of the world and how we move through it as guests, always as guests in someone's house. Perhaps the one memory that best describes our connection came from a moment at the residency when we as residents were talking about being Black and being Brown and in mid-sentence we stopped. It was either I or maybe my friend who asked the question, "Why are we whispering?" Why indeed. I knew then that I would not need to articulate an answer so much as recognize the moment.

I made a meal of matzo ball soup with roasted chicken and a cornucopia of seasonal vegetables. I threw in zucchinis as a commemoration of our time spent together. Who would have thought that a joke about leaving zucchini on your neighbor's porch would lead to this, a friendship forged from the knowledge of our otherness?

My friend this week is visiting, to assume the responsibility of caring for her father. Having witnessed the care and holding that is shared between father and daughter, I stand corrected in calling this a responsibility. This appears to be a privilege, and I was privileged to witness what was between and what moved through.

I am writing this without a story, without a path towards a conclusion. I met a woman I now call a friend. I met her father and held his hand. We ate and we talked and I made a point not to whisper. I told him the story of my mother, and how she lied to keep my family alive. I've held this story for the entirety of my adult life. I shared it with him within a matter of minutes. I showed him a garden grown from the despair of a pandemic. He said it belongs in the book with my mother.

This morning I received an email from my friend. She wanted to pass along a message from her father. She said he dreamed of me from the night before. He wanted to remind me of the garden, of my mother, and of the lie. He referred to it as currency. There is something here that, if written down, I believe I will come to an understanding of, with time. This is not yet a story, a poem, or an essay. For now, I'll call it documentation, of a meal eaten together with my friend and her father. Would it be presumptuous if I were to call her father my friend? It was a dinner shared and free of the concepts of guests and hosts. We ate and we talked. We listened and we found. Perhaps that was all there was. This was all that was needed.

On the walk home

I have a friend on Facebook named Manu. We knew each other from our time in junior high, living in the same neighborhood. We've not talked in person since the eighth grade. He occasionally likes some things I've written and I emoji'd a hug one time when I saw news of someone passing in his family. Will we ever see one another in person again? The probable answer is no. But I will continue to follow along as posts of his daughter's birthdays come through on my feed. I will watch from a virtual distance knowing that his love of his family and his community comes from a place I know to be real. This is enough to know, that Manu is out there, doing his thing.

I knew Manu as Manuli. I knew him on the periphery in junior high, but I knew him just the same. Manuli would go on to be a high school football star. There was talk about him going pro, but aside from hearing this from a distance, I don't really know. I knew him mostly from a single act of kindness where I was only a witness.

There was a boy in school in the seventh grade. His name was Minh and he was new. By new I am referring to those tagged with the ridicule of being FOBs, Fresh off the Boat. In Minh's case, it was via an airplane, but still he was categorized in this culture of otherness as one of the "boat people." I remember growing up and being told that our family were not considered boat people. We were refugees as a result of political hardship and received asylum, a distinction that those arriving in 1975 claimed with a fervor and curious sense of pride.

Being of boat people status, Minh was often singled out, picked on, shamed—for what? For being, for having survived. Even children have a way of knowing and embracing the cruelties of being human. Minh, unlike the others, did not take this sitting down. He fought his way through school on a daily basis and had more wins than losses, at once targeted and feared. And then one day, word was spreading of a beatdown planned for that afternoon at the back fence. Several of the boys had decided that they would put Minh in his place. They said that the FOB would learn what it means to be an FOB. I remember this rumor catching fire through the day and the underlying shame many of us felt for not wanting to be within arm's length, in association.

Minh was not the friendliest kid. He kept to himself. He made little effort to get along. He got word of this rumor as did so many others. He showed no fear of having to fight, and even if he did, he was not one to back down, no matter the odds. He took off his belt and attached it to a combination lock, making a formidable weapon in a matter of seconds. Minh walked his way across the field that afternoon, towards the back fence with a crowd watching and walking along from a distance, close enough to witness a beating but far enough to not get beaten.

Manuli came running from behind; he called out Minh's name. They barely spoke but something, some understanding was exchanged. Together, they walked through the opening at that back fence. No one dared to throw the first punch that day. Minh, with a length of leather wrapped around his hand and a lock dangling from it, and Manuli, with his fists clenched, walked home that day. My writer's memory wants to remember it this way. They repeated this walk for what seemed like a week. I never saw the two of them hang out or eat lunch together or even greet one other in the halls. But that walk across the field was something I'll never forget.

Last I heard, Minh got out of juvie and went to college somewhere on the East Coast. Manuli played football, was the star quarterback. He came to the school I was attending. I heard we lost. I heard that their quarterback was a beast. I didn't attend.

Posting stories and thoughts on social media is a way of giving myself prompts to continue this praxis of writing. I've shared the work because I've come to the understanding that I do not exist or create in a vacuum. My work is in conversation, sometimes with those I consider to be a part of my community, sometimes with the world and all its vastness. This time, I am writing in the hopes that one other person is reading this now. If you are, then let me say what I should have said long ago: Thank you. That's all. Thank you. That's everything.

On the insistence of a future

Why all this effort to write about the past? I am trying to reach for something. I am trying to write beyond my present state of hopelessness. I keep on looking towards a future, but again present conditions lead me to think that there is no hope to be found. The world is burning. This is not hyperbole. At school, children are taught to hide behind doors and under desks, to practice being silent, and to pretend to not be present if the shooter is present, beyond the classroom door. Once we teach this to our children, this drill, I'm afraid the shooter will always be present.

I am comparing my memory as a first grader to that of my godson, now at the same age. There is an innocence and hope in his exultation of the new school year and his new teacher, who does not yell, "Not one bit," he says. I am told by his mother that he has not yet been taught to fear the shooter. I am afraid that this fear will find its way into the thoughts of every child.

My memory of first grade has been reconstructed as trauma, that loving gesture of my teacher who took the liberty to dress me up as the Indigenous other, because she could not help but see an "other." I shared a similar exuberance to that of my godson when I came home and told my mother that I was going to be an Indian in the school's Thanksgiving Parade. Trauma perhaps is the act of looking back and seeing race as an enduring way of life, and still, there was something beyond the trauma that was tucked deep inside.

Why all this effort to write the past? I'm going to be a writer right about now and say that my body is a time traveler. It has a way of knowing the future. It knows just when to take a moment, convert it to memory and tuck it away, and when to dislodge it from within, from the past, as poems and stories and essays and art. Somewhere in these stories of past and otherness, there is the story of wanting and belonging. I still want to belong to a world that is still wanting to be better than what it was and what it is. That's why. And I want it for my godson, whose latest thing is superheroes—that and the promise of matzo ball pho.

On dyslexia or wtf

I grew up in a different time, where I, as an immigrant kid, was all but grown up by the time I was eight. I cooked the family meals by 10, not as a chore but of my own choosing and curiosity. At the age of 12, I was already reading straight erotica and reinterpreting it as gay. All this happened because I was dyslexic. My hope in writing this is that I find my way back to the statements I just made, but that would imply that I actually know where I'm going.

I was never diagnosed with anything more than a cold. I wouldn't receive a diagnosis of dyslexia until I was 40, but I asked that it not be documented, for fear of it being used against me as a teacher. But as a kid, I convinced myself that I was just different, in both existing and understanding. I can say this now with some semblance of confidence, but I did not know it back then. How could I have known? My parents never asked to see my grades. They never said what they expected, but still, they expected that I would go to college, take out loans, and pay my own way towards a better life. That was the base thinking of all things moving forward, that my life was going to be better than the life that came before. But how was I to do that when I could not comprehend?

It took me three times as long to read a chapter of any given textbook. I would stay up all night reading and rereading, only to arrive at not knowing what it was that I had just encountered in words. Language was a nonsensical kaleidoscope of letters and sounds and interrupting images. I never told anyone of my dilemma. Or was it dyslexia? In fact, I did not know of this condition or the term until I thought it was too late. I was in college. I declared my major as Comparative Lit. This was in fact a default decision. I couldn't do science or math or anything that required the deciphering of language. Interpretation was my only option.

In college, I learned how to get by, how to stay above average but never so high up that I would ever be seen. My life in language was about adaptability. I could never keep up with the assigned readings of a class. A book per week per class in a semester of at least four classes as a full-time student meant that I would have to read, at the very least, 20 books in a semester. That was insane and not humanly possible for someone like myself. Adaptability demands creativity. This meant that I would not read a book in its entirety. I would latch myself to a point in the book, state my argument, and doggedly argue that point to a halting conclusion.

A course on Jewish American Literature became a heavy-handed comparative study of the Vietnamese refugee experience. Bible as Literature became Jesus as E.T., where Elliot and Greg and Tyler and Steve were all disciples. There was betrayal and persecution, death and resurrection. I made a case for then-child actress Drew Barrymore as Mary Magdalene. That was a reach, even for my imagination. I made the argument, nonetheless. I got a B–. I graduated from college with just enough, a second-place prize, a publication, to get into grad school.

I chose poetry, again as default. The books were short enough to read, to write if I had to. One day I'll have to, I told myself. Maybe for once, I could get through a book in its entirety. The idea of moving from front to back, from cover to cover was a strange and secret goal for me as a grad student, wanting to be a writer. Adaptability was all about planning, adjusting, doing what you can, and faking what you can't. Creativity and innovation became the catch-all receptacles for my movement through this life of writing and pretending to read. It became my way of hiding my dyslexia or, perhaps more appropriately, denying its existence.

My lack of comprehension of the workings of grammar became the basis of a grammarless writing praxis. My inability to adhere to the tenses of the English language—Vietnamese verbs do not conjugate—became claims to exist simultaneously in the realities of the past, present, and future. The jumbling of language in a poem became a deliberate syntactical choice. What was forgotten on the page became the absence of language. The institution taught me how to be silent. I embraced such teachings. I took shelter in the concept. I hid inside. I convinced myself of this work I was doing, this work of silence, of protest, of shame. I hid this last part even from myself. I am only now finding a way to say this.

How does one exist as a writer when one is filled with the dread of reading? How do I say any of this without feeling like an imposter or sounding like I'm crazy or just trying too hard to be some sort of literary other? Just this morning, I tried to read a chapter from a book. I caught the meaning in bits and pieces and took it upon myself to piece together some imagined understanding. Is this what it means to be dyslexic? To arrive at meaning is always having to risk the vulnerability of interpretation. Is this enough to bring us back to the statements made at the beginning? Was I a grown man at the age of eight? Did I feed my family by the time I was 10? Was I really addicted to porn at age 12? Do I blame this on a condition? Do I diagnose this as living?

On the puzzle still inside my head

In writing about the past, my childhood education or the lack thereof, my fated path to where I am, to who I am, I am thinking about the ways in which I navigated my way here, the constant self-questioning of when to speak up and when not to speak, when to invoke the performance of otherness and when to accept when I've been cast in the role of the invisible, or the countless times I pretended to know, hoping that no one would ask for proof of my knowledge.

◉

When I was growing up in the seventies as a newly arrived immigrant, there were two possibilities. You were either smart and celebrated in your status as a model minority or you were stupid and a thug. How those words and their characteristics found affiliations begins with a willingness to see or in most cases not to see. There was no spectrum to locate, time to bother, or index to help in identifying.

◉

To an immigrant family still consulting the pages of a dictionary, ours was the language of necessity, of this and that. The word "living," an adjective, sat on a page dog-eared for good reason. The reality in my home was simply this. My parents couldn't name what they didn't know. A diagnosis meant being told by the dentist that your child needed braces and the diagnosis that followed was that we couldn't afford them. Sorry, kid, you're shit out of luck.

◉

This need to write about the past and my lack of education, how it is that I became a writer, more specifically a poet. One of my students once sent me a note of thanks. In it, she wrote, "Thank you for teaching me how to lie, cheat, and steal my way into the academy." If only someone could teach me how to cheat, steal, and lie my way out of this damn house, I would write them a note in actual sentences. I would thank them profusely and definitely cook them dinner.

◉

To write about the present moment. To think that my identity, and how I came to see myself, were perhaps a path paved as a series of defaults. I had no choice, no real say in the matter. I couldn't read science or history or math, so I settled on literature. What I didn't understand, I just imagined. I got off the bus, I mean the book. I chose a point and argued that point until it seemed as though I knew. Just don't ask me about what happened at the end. I never made it to an end.

◉

I could never write a series of sentences, like what's happening right about now. So I wrote lines. I wrote poems. I claimed it was an aesthetic choice, an artistic assertion, and a political stance in the English language. Some of that may still hold true. Most of that was the undiagnosed condition of coping as default. I swear on a stack of unread bibles, this is an essay. It is an attempt. For the first time ever, I'm trying to say . . .

◉

I'm doing it again. This essay keeps wanting to be a poem. This sentence is written as documentation. The subject wants to hide in language. This essay wants to be read with clarity. This subject needs to be brought to light. This is dyslexia. This is poetry. It's not supposed to be a poem. This is dyslexia being enacted even as it is being written.

◉

Why now? Why the need to write this now? I have this puzzle still inside. The pieces are stuck inside my head. I'm doing it again. That thing I do when trying to make sense. It's five thousand pieces. The number keeps changing. It's been sitting there all this time. For some reason or another, I cannot seem to throw it out. Perhaps the reason is still inside, that thing I do with the imagination.

◉

I am writing this book. I am constructing this table. It's big enough to spread out the pieces. It's just a matter of doing this work of piecing the fucking pieces together. The numbers keep changing. The words keep changing. This is not the act of circling back, to claim what was lost or to name what was found. Neurodivergence. That's a good word. I'll save it for this generation. The next will have their own way of saying. But as for me, I'm good for now. Then why now? Why the need to write this now? Because this puzzle needs tending to. Because I just need to know this for myself.

On dyslexia and the imagination

What if I told you that I am a writer who did not love literature or poetry, although I did arrive at a kind of love, like loving a pair of shoes given and received as hand-me-downs. They were a little too big and not the right color but with some time, blue, green, and yellow felt markers, wearing-in, waking up to the imagination, they shaped and molded themselves to the contours of my feet in the same way that words and language shaped and molded themselves to the contours of my being. What if I told you, the act of reading a sentence renders the sentence that came before incomprehensible. What if I told you that there is wonder in not knowing. You make things up as you go along. This leads me here to what I am about to say. This is what I've always known. This is who I really am, the default of who I cannot be. Just so you know, this is not an excuse. This is not arriving at a confession. This is a reclamation, a declaration. This is a love letter to everyone who learned the art of faking it, who never made it to the end of the book because reading for them was not and could never be linear. I made up my world along the way. A world of storms and whirling winds that insisted on living in a state of aftermath. Is it any wonder that I survived one shitstorm after another? That is to say, that racism and queerness and trauma and discovery all exist inside this book, in proximity to one another. What if I told you that dyslexia was not a condition that led to coping, but rather an innate ability to survive and sometimes even thrive?

On identity as the sum of all parts

I am a gay man, an Asian man, a Brown man. I am Vietnamese. I am an American. I am an artist and I am a writer. I am the sum of all parts. I move through life with this weight, burden, shame, pride, and privilege at all times. I am informed by these identities.

I came to this country as an immigrant. I inherited this country's history as someone who now identifies as an American. The history of slavery in America is not just Black history. The history of gay struggle is not just gay history. The history of anti-Asian violence is not just Asian history. It is American history, and as such, I've inherited these histories. I have a responsibility to write about these histories as they inform the ways I move through the world. It is a shared responsibility. In this way, writing holds the consciousness of my complicated identity. I have to be present and conscious in my writing because if I am not, I am at risk of being written. I am at risk of being erased.

On offering advice to my younger self

Writing is hard work. Write what is hard. Do the work. Claim your voice. Don't get caught in the performance of it all. If you are angry, write your anger. Break something with your words. Ask questions in your writing. Tell the truth. If that is not enough, state the facts. Imagine. Always write in search of the imagination. I say this as someone who just wrote a book steeped in the difficult real yet is still trying to write the imagined poem.

On Art

On memory as archive (17 Reasons)

Dear Redlicks,
(Corner of 17th St. and Mission)

1) I once bought a round dining table with a label proudly announcing your presence in the world. That was in 1993. "Redlicks," it read. I bought it at a thrift store housed in your husk.

2) I bought it for the fact that the label was intact.

3) I bought it for the history of having visited as an immigrant child in 1975. That same year, your doors shuttered. This memory was reimagined in the years to come, but who would have thought that it would come to this?

4) I bought the table even though there was no truck to transport it.

5) I bought a roll of blue painter's tape. I wrapped this tape around the table's edge. One time, two times, three times, 10. And just like that, it was a wheel.

6) I rolled it across town and up two hills.

7) I made friends with a neighbor who helped carry the table up three flights of stairs. She is still my friend.

8) I placed it in the middle of this room. It was too big, this table. It was too small, this room. But it was mine.

9) That night, I ate my first meal on a table in an apartment in my first home in this city. I think it was Chinese takeout or King of Thai Noodle House. I could be wrong. It doesn't matter.

10) I want to write you this letter. This list as nostalgia for the past.

11) It wants to be a lamentation for all things present.

12) I want you to know how I became an artist on the fourth-floor corner cube behind your brick walls, catty-corner to the adult video store. Still present. Still open. For being human, this is worth noting. The year was 2011.

13) I want you to know that I was evicted, along with 43 other artists, in 2015. I fought the eviction. I lost that fight. I wanted you to know that I fought for the neighborhood. I fought for you.

14) I want you to know I still walk by you every day. I peer in your windows. I look past the hollows of your vacant interiors.

15) There is a startup on the fourth floor. They provide a service. They house blueprints for new developments. I

wanted you to know this. You, who have come this far in seeing.

16) You are history. Forgotten. You are my history. That part of me I'm trying not to forget.

17) I gave the table to a newly graduated student. The exact year I don't recall. I kept the label. It's in a book on a shelf in my home. Still in this city. This matters now. Still. This matters now. Still.

On art and shame

I'm going to write this in all of its complications. This will be the first of many attempts. I am going to begin by first declaring: I cut butterflies from the images of naked white men, deemed by some as lewd. I do this knowingly. And still, I need to write and say this out loud.

I've cut out more than 10,000 butterflies over the course of a decade. I began this practice in response to the artist Damien Hirst's art installation titled "In and Out of Love," resulting in the death of 9,000 butterflies. I began as a protest, matching the killing of 9,000 lives with a corresponding number of male genitals and anuses, all in an effort to say, "What a dick. What an asshole." It seemed appropriate at the time. It seems appropriate even now.

What began as a protest evolved into a practice of meditation. This memory of the body's muscle enacted in the gesture of cutting, moved from anger to mindfulness to mourning for all that was lost in that claiming of art. I surpassed that number of 9,000 butterflies. I stopped counting after 10,000, still this cutting and still this loss that won't stop cutting.

I've adopted the practice of using these butterflies as material for the making of what I see as art. Sometimes I use them to amplify the consciousness of queer identity, as if to say, "It's just the male body; it's just two men having sex." Other times I use them as confrontation in my understanding of whiteness, the white male body as a pervasive presence, whiteness as a conditioned desire, and whiteness as an infestation.

I've been asked on more than one occasion why I only cut from the images of white men. Desire is complicated and fraught with shame. Anger is deep and, thus far, endless. Resentment is a lifetime of endured experiences. Each time the answer is a concoction of equal parts indignation, defense, agitation, and defiance.

Who am I kidding?

I know you are but what am I?

What's it to you?

So what?

Really?

The truth is, no answer is complete. No answer is entirely true. I was asked this question by a white man: "Why do you use only the images of white men?" I am under no obligation to respond. And still, I found myself responding. It's an out-of-body experience where I am witness, yet again, to the white man who insists I explain myself and I see myself succumbing to his expectations. Don't do it, I say. I'm always saying.

Confronted, I said, "It has to do with cutting. I refused to cut into the images of Black and Brown men." Usually, this is where the inquiry ends. But why the refusal? He asked with insistence. "Because I don't like cutting into the images of Black and Brown men." I think my voice was turned up an octave. Again, his insistence on asking why. "Because I won't fragment their images for art's sake, in the act of cutting. We are fragmented enough." The white man continues: "And you are OK with cutting into the image of white men?" "Yes." "And you are OK with the violence?" "Yes."

I am writing this now because I did not say. I was not

quick enough at that moment in my own head. I am writing this now because I want to say: This violence at best is metaphorical violence. It's art. What is a metaphor when in reality? I want to say: What of the actual violence endured by Black and Brown bodies? This question is not art. It lacks the luxury of metaphors.

On the story of the young man in 1963

A plywood board, a model battleship, a red-painted branch, an apple photographed, a young man in his late teens or early twenties, leaning against a barn wall, naked and shy, in black and white. There is both a look of apprehension and strength, as if I could hear him say in his expression, I can do this. I'm going to do this. These disparate ideas came together in an attempt at making something.

At this point in the telling, I will not yet call it art. I did not know this man. I did not taste the apple. This broken branch, I painted it red, in an effort to make it beautiful. I lived through a war at the age of five and thus my obsession with toys that were born of mass destruction. This making began with an image in a magazine from 1963. I am writing this as documentation, as archival practice because this happened. This collage of images, objects, and ideas, I made in an attempt at making art. I hung it on a wall inside my workspace.

I remember that day. It was during an Open Studios event some years ago. I shared my making in the hopes of selling. I will always remember that day when a woman stood in front of this object, looking intently. She smiled. She cried in silence. When I finally asked, "Are you all right?" she said, "Yes." She paused. She said, "I think this man was my grandfather." Her hand extended towards the image. She smiled once more. She asked, "Where did you find this?" Then I remember seeing her walk away.

I have been holding on to this story for some time now. The object is still hanging in my studio. The other day someone asked if my art is for sale. I said, "Yes." They asked if this piece in particular was for sale. It took a minute before I said, "No." I'm still not calling it art. Still waiting in the hopes that she will return. Perhaps another Open Studio. I imagine giving her this object. I imagine the moment when this becomes art.

On the materiality of making art

As a teacher, I am always aware of boundaries. As an artist, I insist on my autonomy. This insistence on separation means that I exist beyond the framing of an academic identity. I make art from found materials, sometimes material deemed inappropriate. In whose world? Not mine. My art is separate from my teaching. I say this as declaration because I want to make my boundaries clear. My art can be seen on the internet, on social media, and as such, moments like this have a way of happening. A student, my student of past or present, in his or their excitement to support my work, will approach me while on campus. They will say something to the effect of: I have something for you, for your art. They reach for something inside their bag and I, in my role as teacher on campus, will say, "Do not pull that from your bag. No." By that, I am referring to a plethora of objects my students will offer up: a fuchsia-colored switchblade, a phallic object of glass, or a stack of vintage gay adult magazines. Whatever the object, whatever the offering, I insist that they keep whatever's inside the bag undisclosed and within the boundaries of teacher and student. For the most part, this is enough of an ending to a story. We share a laugh, sometimes awkwardly and other times genuine. If, in our awkwardness in that moment, if I am not clear, I write this as a note to say thank you. Thank you for the thought. Thank you for the gesture. Thank you for the material, if not for the object or the art. Thank you for this. For the reminder that teaching and art and being have a way of being in proximity, in community. Thank you.

On a hypothetical attempt

This is not an essay so much as a concept. There is a likelihood that this may not come to fruition. In the event of such an occurrence, this written documentation will have to do as representation of the art not yet conceived. Proceed with caution. Do not attempt.

I have a friend who has agreed to teach me how to acquire, build, and operate an AR15 assault rifle for the sole purpose of making art. Once it has served its purpose in the making, this assault rifle will be destroyed, the remaining evidence of its existence will be suspended in resin as a sculpture. All supporting evidence of its construction and coming into being will be preserved as social commentary.

The rifle, when used as a tool of creation, will be aimed and be shot at a piece of 1.5-inch-thick acrylic at a distance of 50 yards, to create cracks and crazes in the material similar in composition to that of a carnation. Shooting a large piece of acrylic enough times, I believe that I will create a still life portrait of a bouquet of flowers. Adding pigments to the crazed acrylic will give it a much-needed burst of complexity and color.

Because the acrylic in its original state would be clear, images can be seen through this object even in its altered state from the AR15's assault and the art's imposition of color and abstraction. I believe it will show itself to be clear, no matter the obstruction, no matter the constructed point of view. What images will I frame from behind the acrylic? There is so much to choose from, so much to remember.

To get to the actual work of creating, I will need to buy the parts online, entirely legal and within my rights. I will need to build this rifle with my own hands. I will need to learn to shoot with some level of competency. The shooting will need to be accurate but still with a margin of consideration, this enactment of chance. One-and-a-half-inch acrylic is bulletproof-grade. It will be expensive. There will be no room for do-overs, no going back to erase what just happened.

I will document this process every step of the way, with photos, receipts, and certificates of authenticity. In a time-lapsed video, I will show my thinking in the process of creation. Why am I doing this? The easy answer would be to say, for art's sake. To claim the duality of making and breaking, and thus proclaim, this is art. There's more to it than just these thoughts. There is the kickback of the rifle butt each time I choose to pull that trigger. There is the underlying fear of doing this work. Why do I want this? What am I saying? There is this invitation for the viewer to arrive.

And then there is this anticipated ending when the making is made and the evidence of its making awaits demise. Will I really destroy what I set out to build? Will I choose to hold on to it for what's to come? For all of the above reasons, this concept might never extend beyond a concept because I am afraid of what constitutes art, the artist, or the object, of what both I and this object are capable of in these fucking times. So much still to grieve and mourn, to arrive at knowing its weight in my hands.

On writing the eulogy of your own making

He sent a casual note to inform me of my art's demise. It was the least that he could do for the maker of the work, he said. It happened while opening the window of his New York City apartment. He was cleaning the apartment on a hot summer day. He went to open his window and there was the sculpture, sitting on the edge of his desk, precariously so, overlooking a corner of Central Park. It was there because it caught the best light, at just the right moment of every sunset of everyday, he said. A single gesture of lifting the window, a shift of his own body's weight, and a sudden loss of balance sent the sculpture to an early end. It shattered on the sidewalk pavement three stories down. I pushed it with my body, he said. I'm sorry, he said. I loved it so much, he said. It was an accident, he said. He ended the note with an attempt at humor. Death really is sudden, he said. He punctuated with a colon followed by a parenthesis.

I imagined him weeping while sweeping up the shattered remains of my creation; I imagined his super yelling from a second-floor window, "You could have killed someone!" And so I imagined reading this sentence: "I'm sorry to inform you that the blunt impact of your 196 used crack pipes neatly packed and gridded into an acrylic box with a photoshopped image of Bambi and a text that read 'crack is wack' struck and killed a pedestrian." I wrote that, just now, to detail and commemorate that which was lost, my art, in the hopes of subduing my own thoughts of anger, violence, and retribution.

Dear friend who is now an enemy who will likely be a friend again: Just give it some time. At the start of this note in response to your note, I could not even bring myself to write your name. I did not know I held such anger, or was it anguish? You were right to write to inform me of the loss—though technically yours, you paid for it in full—of an object I made and sold. I forgot its existence until you told me of its demise. Does one declare an object dead? That would imply that the object in question was capable of dying. That would imply that it once lived. If so, Death came visiting without notice today. Was it art? Was it yours or mine? Or was it the child who came home after being sold and sent away? Or was it the self or some part of myself. I've replaced the art with these few words. Is this now art? Will it live or will it die? Are we there again?

On Breathing

On this obsession with being old

Out of habit, I declare that I am getting old. And the response is inevitable: "You are not old." I'm not saying that with pride, because I've wanted to be older my whole life. When I was 9, I wanted to be 19. I wanted to do what my older brother was doing. I wanted to see it. I snuck into his room. I found the magazines hidden beneath the bottom left drawer. Pictures of men doing things with men. Even at 9, I wanted to know what was happening to me, who I was or, more importantly, who I was becoming. When I was a college student, I rode the bus home on weekends. The same bus driver whose name I never learned would say without prompting, "I'm older than black pepper and she's older than baseball." I rode the bus for that punchline as much as I rode it to get home or to make out with a particular boy at the back of that bus. I have been saying that same phrase ever since. The other day I told my friend that I was old. She asked if I could still touch my toes. I lied and said yes, to which she responded, "You are not yet old." On a different night, another friend, just blurted out, "What is this obsession with being old??" It felt confrontational but loving and so I said, "OK, I'm not that old." We sat in silence until someone said something about the food being too salty. I said, "Black pepper. It needs more black pepper."

On the art of reading the in-between

At the deli counter, I ordered a sandwich, the Tuesday special, meatloaf on rye. I asked for no mayo, light mustard, and said yes to everything else. It was a Tuesday evening, after a long discussion on race, writing, language, and the use of a word, what was heard and what was said. Who said it? Did he say it? Or did he say a word in proximity to the word? All this perhaps is to say that I was tired. To then say that I had no right to be tired. I was hungry. I wanted to be home. I wanted to eat. I wanted to be fed. The man at the counter handed me the parchment-wrapped sandwich. He looked at me with every intention of making eye contact. He said, "I gave you an extra slice of meatloaf." He said it and then he turned his back and walked away. This happened on a given Tuesday probably seven or eight years ago. The Tuesday special is still the meatloaf on rye. I am writing this for the very first time. I am writing what comes next as a series of questions. Why? Was he simply being kind? Did I look like I needed it? Are we not capable of giving? Am I not capable of receiving? Why am I asking? Why do we care? What is this language? What are you saying? Is this everything? Is this it?

On language and how it sticks

Even now, as I am trying to find the language to reflect on the work of becoming, I am encountering my own vocabulary, how it is conditioned and functions in relation to the other. I wrote about a parade of diversity and the other in me had to remind me of my othering. My middle-aged self then portaled back into the first grade when I was assigned the role of the native. I am watching my vocabulary even now. Back in 1976, the identifying word used was "Indian." I believe the term in full was "American Indian." I wore a feather cut from construction paper. The teacher lovingly painted my face. I walked in a single-file line in what I was told was a parade. I remember walking with pride as I waved to an audience of white people. The only Asian kid in pretty much an all-white elementary school made for a pretty convincing American Indian. The next day I woke up and saw the Macy's Thanksgiving Parade for the first time on television. I asked my mother to make a turkey. She roasted a chicken and served it with rice. It would be years before she finally succumbed to the tradition of what she called "the American turkey." Her mashed potatoes came from a box.

On curation, inclusion, and the invitation to come in

For years I hosted a reading series out of my home. I cooked food, something simple but plentiful, made to nourish those in attendance. I left the curation to the community, most of whom were current or former graduate students, some who became friends, even family. I had but one stipulation: that the readings be programmed inclusively. I wanted the readers and audience to represent the reality of our lives. The reality of my life is that I am surrounded by people of many cultures, consciousnesses, curiosities, and ages. I thought this one criterion would be simple enough to fulfill. The simplest of thoughts are often the most difficult of challenges. The reading series, some will say, was the first of its kind. Sometimes 50 or more people packed in my living room listening intently to some other human being with something to say. In this, I believe the reading series was a success. We came together. We listened. We heard. We saw one another. We saw the other. Our success was also our failing. I set the criteria for inclusivity, and over the duration of this endeavor, I stated time and again the need for inclusion. The curators responded diligently. Over the course of those many years, we had everyone from the former mayor of Santa Cruz, to a Tibetan poet writing in the English language, to a Bulgarian teenager who wielded language like a bolt of lightning. A parade of diverse writers came through my home, each saying what needed to be said to an audience of white listeners. Why was the audience so overwhelmingly white? Even now as I am writing this, it occurs to me that parading was, in fact, what was happening in that time. A student once told me that they wanted to come. They rode the bus. They crossed the bridge, and they looked in the window from across the street. They never crossed the threshold to the front door. No matter how much I tried to say, "You are invited, this is your space," the majority of the audience was always white. I invited the world into my living room and the world, as it was, as it still is, came inside. The series ended after seven years. The other day, two friends, two women, one Black, the other Brown, said to me, "We need to bring the readings back. We can do it in your backyard now that you have a backyard." I said I would think about it. And if they were to circle back around, they would have to be reminded and so would I. Curation is not inclusion. I repeat. Curation is not inclusion. The work of including is necessary. And hard.

On the story hidden inside the story

What if I told you that they were friends? Childhood friends who became more than just friends. The older of the two protected the younger. She once fought a boy. She broke his nose. She broke her hand. She said she would kill him if he ever tried that again. Whatever he did, he tried doing to the younger. What if I told you that the younger of the two says that she was the true protector, that it was her job all along? Whatever it took, whatever was needed, she would find a way; she would do her job. Whatever the deed. Whatever the crime. What if I told you that all this was born of the imagination? What if this is all too real?

On not wasting time or language

I live in a building of only three units, classified as condos, according to the barest criteria. We share utilities, insurance, a bank account, and that's about it. I lived with a housemate for many years. He was a renter. He was kind. He took out the trash, recycling, and compost every Monday evening. He did this the entire time he lived with me, for the entirety of the building. This was not an assigned task, it was not part of some rental agreement. He did this on his own. He did this out of generosity. He did this with consideration of contributing to a community. It is worth noting that he is a Brown man. I will not say he did this as a Brown man because he is Brown. That would be presumptuous of me. That would be the Brown man in me. Every once in a while he would forget. This happens. And the trash would build and wait a week. On those rare occasions, I would send a group email to my neighbors; I would make it a point to not include him in the thread. I would gently remind my neighbors of the trash, that it was on us to make sure the trash would go out each Monday evening. Sure enough, the thread extended, as did the tension. And this is what happened, what keeps on happening.

"Hey, can you just ask your housemate to let us know when he is unable to take out the trash?"

No. I can't ask him because it is not his job. "Yes, but what's the harm in asking for an email. It would take a second. He could even start a group text."

No.

"I don't know why this is an issue. It's just a text."

No. I will not ask the Brown person who is renting in this building to text or email the white owners of the building as to when he can or cannot put out the trash. Texting, emailing, or taking out the trash are not conditions to being my housemate. That's not his job. What part of this do you not understand?

I wrote all this and for what purpose? I could have just said, as a Brown man in America, "We are not responsible for your shit!"

On the absolute truth

I spent three days at a friend's home while on a visit to New York. I met my friend's daughter, a precocious six-year-old who has a penchant for games, hugs, and 20 questions. "What's your name? How old are you? Truth or dare? Are you ticklish? What's your favorite animal? Do you have COVID? I dare you to choose dare. Always choose dare. Do you have monkeypox?" Somewhere in between the games and questions, she takes my hands and guides them towards her face. Her eyes, nose, lips, and cheeks cupped in my palms, an unexpected gift of a lasting memory. She tells me she likes the feel of skin. All this before she goes in for a hug that is nothing but the absolute truth.

On the first pebble found inside my pocket

I was gay long before I knew the word. I was in the first grade. I was best friends with a boy named Chad. I wanted to sit by him in class. I played with him at recess and at lunch. He even shared a sandwich my mother made of rice and Spam. And then one day he said, "You want to come over on Saturday?" I felt the thrill of being invited. I ran home that day filled with this excitement. I ran straight into my mother's sewing room. I told her of this invitation. I showed her the paper with his address written in crayon. My mother, though hesitant, could not hide her own excitement, perhaps a little relief in knowing I had a friend.

This notion of going to a white person's house was a first for my mother. It was 1976. We had just arrived in a new town, in a new country. We self-identified as refugees. My mother asked what I would be doing at his house, if I would need to pack a lunch. Was it a birthday party? Did I need to bring a present? What would I wear? Always she worried about what I was wearing. If I was a girl, I'm sure she would have made a party dress. Looking back on my childhood years, I think my mother knew that I was gay before she knew of such a word.

She asked if I needed someone to take me. I think my mother was afraid that she would have to be the one, that she would need to find the words, and that she would need to know this language. I told her not to worry, that I knew the way, that his house was on my way to school. My mother insisted that someone take me to this place. She volunteered my older brother. This was her show of due diligence in being my mother. This was back in a time when my parents were still trusting, especially of white people. Before any of us knew the concept of other, before we as the other developed our penchant for distrust.

That Saturday morning, I got up and got dressed up. I waited for my brother to do the same. We walked together most of the way, and then I said, "I can do this by myself." Something at that moment told my eleven-year-old brother to leave his six-year-old brother. And so he did. I walked the rest of the way on my own. I knew exactly where this boy lived. I knocked on the door and waited outside. No one answered. I knocked again and still no answer. I remember the sinking feeling of disappointment and that was something else I had no words for as a six-year-old. I went down the street. I climbed up a tree with a view of the house. I sat there waiting for the duration of that time I was supposed to be playing that afternoon with this boy I met from school. That was what I told my mother. That was what I pretended to do. I sat in that tree, hidden and intent. I waited with anticipation. I saw a car pull into the driveway. I saw his mother and his father. I saw him going into the house.

I was a six-year-old boy sitting in a tree, contemplating what I should do next. I eventually climbed down. I decided not to knock on the door for the third time. I walked back home that day. My mother asked me how I spent my day with this boy from school. She did not know his name nor did she ask. I said it was great. I made up some lie about some game we played. I said we ate hamburgers and french fries his mom bought from McDonald's. We drank Tang. I told my mom that I liked the way she made Tang better than the way his mom made Tang. This was my memory of that day. Chad stayed my best friend. He didn't say why or what happened, and I never wanted or needed to find a way to ask. On the last day of school in the first grade, we said goodbye in the same way we said our goodbye at the end of each day. I thought I would see him in second grade. That summer, our family moved across town.

I began this story thinking I was writing about the day I discovered that I was gay. It started with good intentions, perhaps even an attempt at some humor. I tried to make this interesting. I convinced myself that this was a story that was worth telling. I've told this story thus far through the eyes of a child. I kept this story for all these years because something inside tells me to keep this memory. I've tried to retell it to the best of my recollections. This was supposed to be the first of many stories about a boy who found his way.

How then did I arrive at this bag of questions? Why did I not go up to that door once more? Why did I not knock? I waited all that time. Was I too proud to show up, having been rejected? Was it rejection? We were only six after all. Was this really the first of many stories about the Brown immigrant boy and the white boy who would grow up to be another white man that I would learn to distrust? How could I have known this as a six-year-old? Why did I concoct such elaborate lies? Why didn't I tell the truth when asked by my mother? Why ask these questions now, now that I know of the things we carry, the things we hold on to. Was this about shame? Is it still? How would I have known? How did I know this as a six-year-old boy? Why have I written this now, forty-seven years later?

On my friend Damian and wondering where he is today

Of the stories I've kept for all these years, one was that of a child wanting to belong. I was in the fourth grade; it seems that memory always leads me back to the fourth grade. Our family had moved to a new neighborhood. We did a lot of moving back in those days. My father was obsessed with leaving the image and the sounds of the ice cream truck in the rearview mirror. My parents bought a house. An ugly house in an ugly neighborhood dubbed by the Vietnamese neighbors "Xom Rac." Translated, it meant "the garbage neighborhood," because our houses were built on landfill once designated as the city's dumping grounds.

I was in the fourth grade, so that would make me 10 years old. I was eager to make friends. I had Vietnamese friends and Mexican friends and Black friends aplenty in the fourth grade. My school was the gathering grounds for everyone poor and everyone immigrant back in those days. The neighborhood was what we would call "diverse" today. Back in those days, it was the reality of being poor, frugal, and driven enough to buy our way into some version of the American Dream, which, for my parents, was the idea of paying a monthly mortgage. For me as a child, it was to have friends, white friends. Like so many of my Vietnamese and Mexican and Black friends, I wanted to have white friends. We were conditioned from a young age to adhere to the caste system of guests and hosts, to feel that we were just visitors, passing through. In the neighborhood, there were three white families amidst a world of Samoans, Vietnamese, Filipinos, Mexicans, and Blacks. These three families all lived within walking distance of one another. They all knew each other. Their children were friends and they all had boys about my age. I wanted so bad to be their friend. I learned to play football, ride a skateboard, shoot bumper pool, all in an effort to play along. I played on their front yards, in their opened garages, and every so often they would come to my house, knock on the door, and ask if I would come out to play. My mother wouldn't always be so trusting. She would ask about homework and chores and who these boys were and who their parents were. She would always agree after a back-and-forth of pleading, negotiating. She would always tell me to stay outside so that my brothers could find me. One day, my mother warned me without mincing words: don't go wandering into white people's houses.

This story I thought was about me as a child, that one time when I played inside one of their houses. The boy owned an Atari 2600. He had just gotten *Space Invaders*. We played for hours that afternoon. When I returned the next day, my three white friends and I were met by the mother of the friend. It was her house. She spoke in a calm and deliberately stern voice. I remember when she addressed me directly, her voice slowed down even more, as though she was making a concerted effort to make sure I understood what she was saying. "Someone took some money from my purse. It was five dollars. I am giving you all a chance to return it now." One by one, we each denied any wrongdoing. And then, one by one, they each accused me of being the thief. I remember that woman kneeling down, taking my hands, and asking, "Did you take the five dollars?" I remember pulling my hands away, wanting to go home. That was the last time I was inside any of their homes. I went home that day trying to pretend that nothing had happened. It took but one question from my mother, and all the tears came flooding through.

I thought this story was about my mother, who walked with me to their house after dinner that night. She handed the woman an envelope. She said this to me when we got home: "You never go into white people's homes." Even to this day, 43 years later and well within my middle age, I can hear that woman. I can hear my mother. "Did you take the five dollars? You never go into white people's homes!"

I've written about this story several times before. I've written about the white boys in the neighborhood, the mother of that one white boy, my mother, that walk my mother and I took to and from that white woman's house. I've written this story as a way of putting down the anger, as a means to enact the rage that was lodged in muscle and memory. I've written about the shame of being wrongly accused, the shame that is transferred from son to mother, mother to son. I wondered if my accusers, the white woman, the white boys, the boy who stole the five dollars, I wondered if they ever felt the shame, the shame I felt for being accused, for being Brown. I am revisiting this memory so as to write about the day that followed.

I walked to school the next day, along with the three white boys, who again accused me of stealing five dollars. I remember sitting in the classroom, overcome with anger. I remember crying, enacting some kind of physical violence on some inanimate object. What I have not written about is this: the boy who sat next to me, I remember him asking if I was all right. He raised his hand. He told the teacher that I was hurt, that I was crying, that someone must have done something to me. I remember his name. His name was Damian. I remember him whispering something along the lines of, "I can beat them up. I'll fight for you." We never fought anyone. We never talked about what made me cry. We were friends in the fourth grade and then we went to different schools. As I am writing this now, I am remembering the one time when we ran into each other at the mall. We were in our twenties. We recognized one another immediately. He was married and I was not. He had two kids and I was in school. We talked about what little we remembered, our teacher Mrs. Brooks. He said his son goes to that school, where she was now the principal. We talked and then we said goodbye.

Why have I not written about this boy until now? Perhaps I thought this story was about the anger and the shame and the hurt and the othering. Perhaps the mind has a way of compartmentalizing, when really this story is about the love and the care of that child who sat next to me in a classroom in the fourth grade. His name is Damian. He is Black and I am Vietnamese. This detail means everything to the writing and rewriting of this story, to the journey of this memory and its arrival, to me.

On breaking the fall

To say that life is fleeting is to invoke a cliché. But then again, what is a cliché if not the truth repeated to the extent that it becomes numbing, losing meaning in its acute invocation. To say that life is fleeting is the equivalent of being jabbed with a butter knife. You do not expect it to break the skin, until one day . . .

I am writing this now because I have been getting weekly reports about the failing health of a dear friend's partner. To read the letters as reports written in this matter-of-fact way, to cut to the language of what needs to be said, what is needed in such times, is to know the helplessness and distance from the pain that comes with penning such cries to be seen, positioned as reports. I have written notes in response in the hopes of reassuring this friend that I am here should she need my support in any capacity. I send them and then I go about living as I do, in a haze, at a distance from the other, at a distance from myself.

At the risk of writing another cliché, I want to know that I am living with intent, with urgency, that every minute of every day counts. The other day, I spent almost three hours on a park bench across the country, looking back, talking with a childhood friend. We talked about conflicting knowledge of the past that somehow leads us back into the present. He was an artist who became a husband, then a father. He said that was so long ago, the idea of making art is now distant and a dream belonging to a different version of himself. I said I was not trusting of dreams.

I did not want to go to college and here I am a teacher at a college. I hated museums and here I am making things that aspire to live and die in museums. He said, "You are living the dream." I said, "Dreams are clichés." He said, "I've given up wants for a binding contract. A wife, two kids, and everything that comes with that and all the terms of maintaining what's agreed upon." I said, "I am living a lie." He said, "You are writing a book, *The Book of Clichés*." We laughed. We sat in silence and then we went back into the comforts of childhood memories. This seems strange and nonsensical to claim, but this is the urgency and intent I am talking about. I was an old man one minute full of regrets and in the next, a boy living on Lantern Court, burning with curiosity. That the past has a way of becoming, awakening the present. To my friend whose partner is dying or has died in the near or distant future, know that arms are extended in the hopes that I will catch you. And should I fail in my attempt, I will do my part to break the fall.

On the constraint of not writing angry

I am 57 years of age. I have been a writer most of my adult life and I am only now finding a way to write this. What exactly is this? It is the unlearning of language, packed and arranged into a container meant to convey opacity. This hinting at the meaning is not without purpose. It saved me those times when I needed to hide. It gave me the illusion of having a voice. This opacity is the silence that sells itself as a form of protest. The lack of language on the white page was supposed to be the withholding of meaning, as though my contribution is of value to those whom I am depriving of my voice. This is the opacity of meaning between the writer and the reader. Let me say this with certain clarity: I am referring to this Brown writer. I am talking about the white reader who hides in spaces like the academy. This is the hope of the self when trying to be seen. But what if the site of such exchange conditions you to this silence, where silence becomes the condition of living, of being?

I came to a university as a student to find my voice, only to be told my voice was best rendered when shrouded in silence. I was led to believe that silence is what they will hear, my silence as anger and protest and craft and performance. My silence as an otherness that they are willing to archive. Silence as the quietude of existing as a Brown body in the white space of the academy. This is the opacity of my Brown self, calling myself a scholar or writer or teacher or professor. I stayed in this university to proliferate this thinking, thinking I would teach others to write in silence; this work of silence is the opaque body in the academy. Seen but not really meant to be seen, heard, and read, but on the condition of being metered and interpreted. "Truong is nice but small in comparison." Written in the notes, as a qualifying evaluation, this is the white academic's learned interpretation of the other. This is me leaving this white man's page.

At 57 years of age, I am leaving this place, this silence, this opacity behind. I am unpacking what I thought were my belongings. This is me saying to the white academic who stupidly called me "small in comparison": Go fuck yourself. This is me at 57 years of age. I am writing this, saying this loud and clear.

On the essay as a series of questions

Can anger be in proximity to the memory of my father, in the same way he existed in proximity to a war? Can it sit next to the honoring of my mother? Was it present when, as we fled Vietnam, she sat down with no intention of standing up? Or was it the kindness of a stranger whose name I did not know. You asked that question: "Are you all right?" The hope is that you will read this one day, you will remember that exchange, and you will find a way to tell me your name. Or is this just a matter of imagination? Would it be all right if I imagine your name? Can anger follow the love of a child who placed my hands upon her face, who gifted me the memory of her Herculean hug? Would anger be anger having witnessed this child? Can this anger coexist with joy and loss and love and despair? Yes, there is bound to be despair somewhere in this book. That would be typical of a book, no? Can the source of this anger find its way to the pages of this book? If so, why? Can this child take comfort in the story of my aunts? Can she and they find common ground? Can they claim they did it for the wanting of the other's love? Can someone white identify as other? Can they make peace with the child version of myself? Can I hold on to this past, in myself, in the past? Can an essay exist as a series of questions? Is this enough of an attempt at answering? What do you say when someone says, "But he, but she is just so angry?" When can I put this bag of bricks down? Where is there a window that I might find a way to look in, to break in, to tether this brick to a brick made of anger and throw it through a pane of glass? Is this a crime if evidence shows this brick was thrown from within the house? I guess it depends on who's filing the charges. Is this abstraction? Am I losing clarity? Did this fall back into a poem? Is this obstruction? Is this not the point? Is this a story? Is this an essay because it attempts? Why this constraint of writing without anger? Why am I holding on to this anger? Is anger necessary? Is forgiveness lurking nearby? How does one recover from a lifetime of anger? How do I let go? Put down? Is this an addiction? How do I hold on to this anger? How?

On rooting

If there was anything positive about the pandemic, it was that I found the part of myself that I did not know existed. I have a love for plants and nature that I misconstrued as loathing before this isolation of being. My backyard was a graveyard for old bicycles, remnants from a housemate who proved to be a hoarder. I asked him to leave, and in his haste and anger, he left me buried beneath the bounty of his hoard. My garden was also covered in weeds and trash. I was conditioned, if not content, to live with these ruins. That was until my friend insisted on giving me this gift of a garden, a place of manifestation. He weeded and tilled until the earth came to life. He mapped out a world, created paths knowing I have this need to wander, to hide, to share in this burden of living. He constructed a gate that kept the world out, that keeps this secret tucked inside. I spent those days that became months and years digging and planting and watering and caring. I potted and repotted, clipped and trimmed, arrayed and arranged and worried and wallowed in the pure wonderment of it growing. Will it grow? How will it grow? Will it outlive me? This began as an idea born of a friend's desire to give. He wanted to give me a space to sit and think. I am doing just that. I am thinking of this gift of friendship, how little we know of what it means, of how and when we give this to the other, of how it saves us in ways the giver will never truly know. So that you know, so that it's clear, this essay follows an essay on anger.

On meeting your "friend" for the very first time

The other day I opened a message on one of those social media platforms. The message came from someone I knew. It read, "I can't believe our friend is gone . . ." There was a link attached to the message. I clicked it and then immediately clicked the little red dot at the upper-left corner of the screen. I was hoping it didn't stay open long enough to allow for any form of computer hacking. I was proud of myself for thinking I had pulled my hand away from the fire just in time.

Who died? Who sits around and thinks of these things? As the day progressed, and by "progressed," I mean in a matter of minutes, I started getting messages from friends on this social media platform. "Hey, Truong I think you got hacked." "Hey, Truong, they got you, my friend." "Did you mean to send this?" A slew of messages came flooding in, notably from friends of a younger age group, all doing their due diligence in telling me that I had been compromised electronically.

This led me to post a public message on the site with a bold headline that read, "PLEASE READ!" My public post stated that I had been hacked. I asked that everyone ignore my previous message and avoid the link. I wrote it as a matter of fact. I tried to sound direct, conscious, and strangely dignified, all in an effort to veil the reality of that posting, this moment when I became that guy, the vulnerable uncle who goes and wires a stranger money because some distant relative is stranded in Tunisia, without money and passport, and is desperate to get home. For the record, I thought about it, but then I heard that my cousin was at the time in Wisconsin.

Who sits around and thinks of this stuff, and how did I get to be this guy? My public posting was the equivalence of a walk of shame. I was dumb enough, or in this case, old enough to be manipulated emotionally with just a few choice words. As the day progressed even further, I began getting messages of a different kind, "Who died?" "I hope it's not someone I know." "I can't open the link. Can you resend it? Who died?" "Who? I can't take any more bad news."

These messages came from friends and acquaintances, most of whom were 50+ years of age. I wrote back to each of these individuals. I said, "Hi." I asked them how they were doing. I apologized for having exposed them to a hacker. I found myself reconnecting with some friends I'd not seen since the pandemic and others I'd never met or talked to in person. Someone asked, "How's your mom doing?" Another joked, "What's a hacker?"

And still another responded. I didn't know this person before that day. We've made plans to meet for coffee. I'll end on this note. "Hello, my friend. Not to worry. I click on those things all the time. At my age, you want to know who left the room. God forbid I click one day to find my name in a sentence in that message. Getting hacked is just a reminder that we're still alive :)"

On how a friend becomes family

He makes a point of saying that he was never my student. He was my teaching assistant. This distinction is important to him, so now it's just as important to me. We met and became friends out of common interest. We played tennis together. We never actually played a game of tennis, but we enjoyed the ease of communication that came with the act of hitting a ball back and forth and back and forth for hours at a time. The year we became friends, I was turning 40. There was going to be a surprise party for me. I was not supposed to know. Dan was invited. He accidentally told me when he called to say he couldn't attend. He was on his way to Florida that weekend to make arrangements for his father's funeral. He called me while at the airport. He wished me a happy birthday. He told me of his father's passing. It was unexpected. He was supposed to be going there a week later for an entirely different purpose. He was going to be his father's best man. I said I was sorry for his loss. He said he was sorry he couldn't be at the party.

Dan and I were more than just friends. We shared an art studio. We collaborated in our desire to reimagine the world. I was amazed that a Jew and a Vietnamese, straight and gay, 17 years apart in age, could connect in ways that I could never have with my brothers or my nephews. I remember this one time when we were working on a show together, and I chose to stay home to watch a game. It was the playoffs, and the Niners were on the verge of a Super Bowl berth. I didn't go into the studio to work that Sunday afternoon. The deadline for the show was getting closer. We didn't do the gym, as Dan and I had planned.

We did have dinner later that week. He was still angry. He said that I was not serious about the work, about my health. He was raising his voice from across the table. Something happened at that table. Something was left unsaid that night. We stayed friends. I flew to Jamaica to be at his wedding. I officiated the exchange of vows. I played the part of internet-certified Minister Tran. During the ceremony I said, "and with no authority whatsoever, I pronounce you Dan and Rahel." I'm sure that didn't sit well with some of their relatives.

Yet that was a memory I hold with great care. I was asked to pronounce my friend's name and that of his partner, to announce their union in life and in love. I'm writing this essay. I'm keeping it here inside this book, should the time come when someone would ask, "Why is he here? How is he the executor? Why does the white guy have a say in the matter?" Something was left unsaid on that day and at that table. That something was care. My friend cared enough to raise his voice. I cared enough to listen. I heard him say "yes" to a question I would ask him some years later.

On carrying the weight of another's story

There are times when the moment becomes a memory, and tucked inside is a story that wants to be told. Sometimes those stories are not our own, and still we carry the burden of knowing their weight. I remember the phone ringing like it was yesterday. I remember the cousin calling to ask if her family could borrow my father's camera. The funeral was going to happen soon. Their family needed to document what happened here. To send back there, back when we thought that home was there. It was still there.

In hindsight, what happened back then was a twelve-year-old boy found a gun beneath the front seat of his father's car. He was playing with it while his father was driving. The gun went off and my friend went missing. I told his cousin I would ask my father about the camera. And then she said this. She called that day asking for a camera but really she called asking and declaring this: "Have you seen him? If you see him, tell him to come home. The police say it was an accident. Tell him to come home. We want him to come home." I'm still looking for permission to write, I'm looking for a room in a country still with the hope of finding a home, that I might find a way to say.

There are no further details to this story, nothing that is my right to share, my place to say. No rumors of the past that need recounting. There is just this memory of a phone call. There is this weight of all these years of wondering about my friend, if he ever found a way home.

On crafting an essay of the American story

In some version of this story somewhere in the past, present, or future, someone would have to assume the role of the villain. Would it be the woman judged for her wants and indiscretions? This was America, the 1970s, after all. Given the pre-existing conditions of this narrative, she could only be one of two possibilities. Would it be the husband because he was othered, betrayed, made to feel lesser, and driven to violence in a fit of jealousy? Again, as a reminder, this is still America. Would it be the boy, privileged and white, barely out of school but still in his teens, still acting on his teenage impulses? Given the cast of characters, the time and the place, he was more likely to remain as he was. The concept of victim and villain as one and the same was not yet conceived. Life was simpler back in those days. Would this villainy land on the grieving parents, who wanted justice for their son, or was it retribution, or was it peace that they wanted all along?

◉

This story was the stuff of R-rated scripts from the '70s and '80s. If ever made into a movie, it would have been a comedy played at theaters at the mall. The escape through the second-floor window, naked and embarrassed as audiences laughed along. The teenager ran down the street in the middle of the day. His embarrassment turned to pride in celebration of his teenage conquest. Were we laughing at the man, too angry and lacking in language at that moment to be dignified? Was I laughing at myself? Were we laughing at the woman portrayed with some measured level of alluring modesty and still exuding her Asian exotic otherness. Though underage, my friend and I had our ways of sneaking in. We watched such movies, intently. My friend was always looking to laugh.

⊙

This was supposed to be a comedy. Something to look back on, to chalk up to youthful indiscretion. That everyone would find a way forward, the teenager with his whole life still ahead, the newly arrived immigrants with their story still to be lived and written. There was never supposed to be any depiction of grieving parents. No funeral. No trial. No sentencing and no crime. No waking from this dream of the American nightmare. He had no business being there. No matter the reason, no one was supposed to die that day. Had the husband not forgotten the lunch she packed him for the night shift. Had he not circled back. Had the teenager not hidden in the closet. Had he not forgotten his underwear while in a hurry to hide. Had they not worked together at the supermarket. Had he not asked. Had she said no. There would be no story wanting to be told, no story waiting to become.

⊙

The young man died of a stab wound that day. The husband surrendered just as quickly as he committed the crime. He pleaded guilty for having temporarily lost his mind in that moment. The parents of the young man asked the judge for leniency on behalf of their son's killer. He said he was sorry. They said they forgave him. That was all that was said between the two parties. The woman gave birth to a healthy baby boy. She and the child moved north to be closer to her family. She never visited her husband in prison. He wanted it that way. He got out a few years later. They reconnected. They remained a married couple. He loved the boy. By all accounts, he was a good father. He saw the boy go off to college before passing away from a heart attack.

◉

Why is this story being told? Why now and why this impulse to frame it as a script, to imagine it as a movie, a comedy for that matter? Remember that kid I went to the movies with for all those years? He is the son inside this story. He is my friend. We keep in touch from time to time. He called me up the other day. We talked. We caught each other up on the happenings of our lives. I told him I was a writer. He told me this story. He told me about meeting his grandparents for the first time. And then he asked me if I would write about it, and still I asked him for permission. He said, "You're the writer. Just promise me this. Make me laugh if I'm going to read this essay or this story. You call it what you want. I just need to laugh at what comes before the story of me."

On the missing bag

Back in May 2022, I met up with a former student to catch up over a lunch consisting of tacos and horchata. She insisted on treating. She said she was all grown up now and that she could afford to take her favorite professor out this one time. A moment like that makes it worthwhile to call oneself a teacher, even if you've not had a raise in the last 10 years. It is the reassurance that your student is thriving, or, if not thriving, then at least OK in that moment in that exchange.

We ate at a taqueria on Haight Street. We sat outdoors along the sidewalk, where I hung my leather bag from the dining chair's back. We talked about her many jobs and the desire to keep on writing. We talked about my suspect health and the reality of growing old. She said that I was not old, and then we spent a good half-hour debating the logistics of being old. We talked about my latest obsession, this newfound love of nature and gardening. As she's one of the strongest human beings I know, I asked her to help me plant a 13-foot dogwood tree that was leaning up against a wall in my backyard. After planting it, we sat in the backyard admiring our handiwork. We rewarded ourselves with a couple of beers. We circled back to the subject of writing. I wanted to show her the book I was currently trying to read.

I looked for my bag and it was then that I realized I left it on that seat outside the restaurant. By the time we got back there, the bag was gone. The rest of that day, I tried to convince her that it was only a bag. Deep beneath this outward display of no-big-deal, I was devastated. I had coveted that bag long before I took the plunge and splurged on it as a treat for myself and, in fact, it was a source of great pride. Everywhere I went, someone would say something kind about the bag. How is it that kindness comes by way of an object? It made me feel, strangely enough, like I was something other than myself. I am a writer and an artist, but for some reason, I needed this bag to hold my belongings and my identity as both. Its worn-in characteristics conveyed a history, a lived experience of someone else, someone worthy of being called a writer or an artist. Why did this matter? Why did I put all that in a bag?

In the weeks that followed, I reminded myself constantly that it was just a bag. I looked for a replacement online but then decided to just let it go. Why am I compelled to write these disparate narratives in the hopes of finding a worthy story? I know that there is something here, something inside this bag, inside these sentences that I am still trying to bring to the surface.

I traveled east that May. I lectured at a university, read at bookstores, and taught a workshop to a group of writers. I entered into these spaces with my book in hand, my thoughts scripted, and no bag to hold my identity as a writer. I stayed in a hotel and then at a bed and breakfast where I was always seated at a table by myself. To be fair, all the guests or groups of guests were seated with their people. It would have been strange to be seated at any of the various groupings, the father and son on a bird-watching expedition, the newlyweds from the next town over, or the family with their teenage children texting on their phones. How did I know this? I was told by the woman who ran the B&B. Why was I told? I'm not sure why, but I have to admit, I was curious. They were all white and apprehensively friendly. They offered hellos, and I in turn made it a point to say goodbye. Somewhere in between, we exchanged a question here and there. I was acutely aware that I was alone and wanting to be invisible.

I came home after a week of traveling. I had forgotten about the bag again. A letter was waiting upon my arrival, written with the shaky penmanship of someone older or struggling, someone living with the weight of living. Inside the envelope was my credit card and ID, no cash or wallet, and a note that read, "My name is Heidi. I found your bag. Do you want it back? Call me if you do. You look handsome in your picture." This letter, which read like a ransom note, brought me hope and a sense of familiarity. I went to bed that night thinking I was home.

Again, I pause to ask the question. Why am I writing this and what is the point? I still don't know, but something compels me to put words down on this page, to wander in search of a worthy narrative, an attempt, always an attempt.

I called the number provided in the letter the very next morning. I spoke with Heidi. I thanked her for the letter, for returning my credit card and ID, for the promise of returning my beloved bag. She said she would get it back to me but she needed a few days, a week maybe. I ended the phone call with an appointment to call again in one week's time. Some part of me knew I needed to play this with a level of measured calmness. I needed to acknowledge mentally the precarious nature of this interaction. I concocted a story of the bag as a gift from my father, not long before he passed away. This was a lie that I made up on the spur of moment. I had hoped that it would serve as an incentive to locate and return my missing bag. I told a lie about my father to a stranger I'd yet to meet. Maybe I am writing this now to come clean.

There is something more to this narrative that's telling me to keep writing. Where am I going with my words? The truth is, I still don't know. I called Heidi a week later, exactly at noon, as scheduled. I tried for some semblance of casual banter. I asked how she was doing. I told her of my excitement and how I shared the news of her kindness with my friends. I then asked her if she had found the bag. And not surprisingly, her answer was "no." This reach for a conversation quickly turned into a confrontation. "Who did you give my bag to? What is this person's name? Why did you give it to this stranger? And where and when did you give it to this person? This was my father's bag. You had no right to give it away." By this point in the exchange, I was losing my patience. I was starting to raise my voice. I had convinced myself of my own lie. This was now my father's bag. I wanted it back at whatever the cost.

She said she had given it to a stranger so that he would leave her alone. She said she had given it to him to carry some things and that she gave it to him at the corner of 6th and Market Street about three weeks back. I mentioned the prospect of looking for it myself, of filing a police report. I asked for his name. She quickly denied knowing his name. She asked that I not file a police report. She asked for another week and then she told me to have a little faith. Something in the way she said it told me the truth of my defeat. I asked her to stop her search, to not put herself in danger, that 6th and Market was not a place to wander about alone. I asked that she let it go, and in that instance, again, I told myself to let it go. Heidi said that she was still going to try. To which I said, "Please don't." Our discourse ended. Writing this now, I realize I've written thus far to arrive at this knowledge of my shame. Did I use my tone in this way to intimidate another in that moment? Did I assert my authority? Did I become the bully by way of wielding the English language? I've written this story. I've arrived at an ending. The bag is back in my possession. I thanked Heidi on the phone and in person. I brought carnations at her request. I brought her chocolates. I said, "Thank you." I lost the note with her number written on it. I have no way of staying in contact. I've written all this to say I'm sorry.

On reliving the same story

I woke up that morning thinking, for someone in the middle of writing a book, I have nothing to say. Strangely, I thought that was a good thing. I gave myself a much-needed break. I took the subway. I got off at the last L stop, just as directed by Siri, this voice of a woman who lived on the phone. She walked with me the rest of the way. She said, "You have arrived." Siri was new back in those days. If she were human, I wondered if she would be labeled as immigrant, documented, guest, or newly arrived.

I went into the museum. I was doing that thing of being cultured in the big city. Twenty-five dollars to look but not touch. Ridiculous, I thought, and there I was, looking at art, being told to please step back, stay behind the designated lines, and please wear your backpack in front of you. Somewhere in between another Warhol and a white woman's rendering of what it means to be Black and grieving, something got caught somewhere in my throat. I started coughing in a crowded room. I immediately made my way towards an exit. I went out to the museum's mezzanine. I sat down on a bench. I covered my mouth with a scarf. I allowed myself a full-throated cough to clear my throat. I covered again. I coughed. And then it happened. An older white museum attendant approached. He instructed me to cover my mouth. He said this as though I was a child. Needless to say, I was already doing this.

The moment happened and I was there, seeing it happen outside my own body, as though I were a witness to a loop in my own life. "I know." I said, "I am." I said, "Really?

What are you really trying to say?" I really wanted to know what he was thinking in that instance of his approach. *He's spreading germs. They have bad hygiene. His kind, they don't cover when they cough. They chew with their mouths open. His kind, they don't belong in places like this, always his kind.* He looked as if he wanted to say "shame," but he didn't respond, not even a word. He turned away. He spoke into a handheld device. And that was when I said, "You fucking racist." If you are frightened now, you are thinking, this is a bit of an overreaction, he was just doing his job, you need not go any further. If this feels painfully familiar, like it happened last week or you read it in the news or you think it ends with someone being arrested, stay with me. Share with me in this endeavor. I was sure he heard me, as did the people walking by. And so knowing who I am and where I was and who he represented in that moment, I left that museum of my own volition. I was not about to let them walk me out or talk to me in that condescending, dismissive yet cautious, *please don't make this about race right now* tone. Was it defeat or victory I felt, having said what I said, then scurrying out? I retraced my path back into the subway. I rode the train. I missed my stop because I was lost in my thoughts about what had just happened. I asked Siri for directions on my walk to get back home. She was direct and unexpressive. Perhaps angry still, or weary, or desperate, or just plain done, I found comfort in her voice. Her even, measured way of speaking, I heard as kindness, and free of judgment. She said, "You have arrived." If only that were true.

On writing an addendum

I want to note that the preceding story was first written as a poem in a time before COVID but long after SARS. It has gone through several revisions. I removed the bits about patient zero, the re-emergence of SARS, and any direct references to New York City. There was just no room for the imagination. I revised until it was no longer a poem, nor was it much of a story. There was just me left somewhere in the strangeness of that city and that world, trying to get back to a home that was not mine. There was still the anger. That part never seems to go away, even when the constraint was to wake and write without the anger. There was this shift to the second person, the pronoun "you" because, again, there are times when you needed to see yourself. There is this shift to the present because you see this is still happening. You tell yourself that this is stupid because you are running out of words, this need to write about this happening still, the old white man, the need to imagine this narrative to the end. You tell yourself you've written this story before. You've written it in this book and every book you've ever written. You witnessed the old immigrant man coughing on the bus; you saw your father as that old man. You've seen the old white man before as a young man, as a white woman. You see yourself. Even now, even at this age, asking that question: Why does it always have to be about race? You want this to be your last response, but you know. You just know that you will live and write this story again. And so you write this as a reminder. Remember, even when it's not about race, the truth is that it will always be about race.

On the joy of seeing Suu

I am writing this without her consent or permission. I trust that she would be all right if she knew. A few years back, the local news made a short film about her life. It celebrates her remarkable story of being a single woman in San Francisco. It revealed the story of her daughter, who was killed by her husband, Suu's son-in-law. She whispers on camera, still with a hint of fear, that he's in jail. Her daughter left behind three young children that Suu raised as her own, on her own. In her narration of this life, Suu declares that she is a single mom. She says it's very difficult. That, in itself, is a remarkable fact, but she neglects to mention that she is, in reality, a single grandmother. The coupling of those two words feels like a gut punch whenever I consider the gravity of her endeavor. Let me state this with as much clarity as is possible in the English language. This is a single grandmother who raised her three grandchildren after the death of their mother in the most tragic of circumstances. She did this as a waitress. She did this well into her 60s, as someone who worked for the city, sweeping and cleaning the streets of a San Francisco neighborhood.

Suu's story is not my story to write. I am only retelling what has been written and filmed and documented; much of this was told in her own words. Suu carries a laminated clipping of her story from the local newspaper. She keeps it tucked away in her cleaning cart. She is proud of the write-up, and rightly so. She's shared it with me on more than one occasion. The story I'm writing today is not much of a story. There is no arc, no real conflict, no overcoming of any struggles. Should these words ever find their way into a book, I hope to upholster the cover in a protective layer of plastic. I'll present it to her one day while eating a lunch of banh mi together or maybe as I'm walking by her side as she sweeps her way up Irving Street. I think she'll like it in all its ordinary details. I think she'll like it because it's our story. This story is just an ongoing conversation between two people who happen to know and like one another. Perhaps I could even venture to say that we love one another. Perhaps that's why I want to write this story.

Our first conversation began 30 years ago. I know this for a fact because it happened during the first meal I ate as a resident of San Francisco. It was a bowl of pho at a restaurant named Henry's Italian and Freedom Pho, just down the street from my first apartment on 10th Avenue. It was actually Henry's Italian and Pho Tu Do. Tu Do translated means "freedom" in Vietnamese. Freedom Pho is just too good a name to not be included in our story.

She was the only waitress at this restaurant on that day. They were short-staffed, which was the reason she was running frantically with steaming hot bowls of pho from the kitchen to the tables. I was afraid, deathly afraid that I would be a witness to a fatality, an accident involving a flipped tray and cascading, crashing bowls of piping hot soup. I told her to stop! I don't know what came over me or where I found the courage as a 23-year-old to say what I did. I said it all in Vietnamese in the language of a 10-year-old boy, "No one's going to die or starve to death if they don't get their pho right this minute." She paused before responding in Vietnamese. She called me "em trai."

Translated, it means "little brother." She asked a question. "Is little brother worried?" Rhetorical or not, that was the beginning of our conversation. It is still happening even now. I hesitate to call her my friend, even though I've grown to love her like a sister or an auntie. This hesitation is because I have never had her over for a home-cooked meal. I tell her of my Vietnamese cooking prowess and she jokingly responds with doubt and gentle ribbing. Every once in a while, I'll remind her of this promised meal, but I sense some hesitation on her part and thus I hesitate out of respect.

I ran into her in the bric-a-brac aisle of a thrift store on Haight Street today. After more than two years of isolation, a global pandemic, and an overwhelming year of constant news of anti-Asian violence, I heard her voice and then I heard her say, "Em trai." She recognized me through my mask. She didn't call me by my name but rather the name she gave to me, "Little brother." That voice, how could I ever forget that voice? She immediately launched into her diatribe of this and that and questions and memories. All this, of course, in Vietnamese, clocking in at record speed. How's your mother? Is she still alive? Remember Henry from Pho Tu Do? I heard he went home. She announced her ripe regal age of 73. She asked me if she still looked good, and by "good" she meant healthy for her age. She then turned to the topic of her grandkids. She shared a plethora of pictures. This one just turned 32. Look how handsome he is! This one graduated just this year. She flipped through the images with the technical agility of a seasoned teenager. I told her I was worried, and before I could find the right words in Vietnamese to finish my thought, she interrupted with a joke: "You thought I was dead?" She laughed at her own joke. She made a point of telling the Vietnamese woman behind the counter that I was her little brother and that I was a professor at the university. "You see how healthy I am?" she asked for the second time. She told me that she went back to work, still at the same place and still on the same street. She gave me her schedule of exactly when and where she would be sweeping. I told her I would find her and bring her lunch. She said she was on a diet. She laughed. I thought she was joking, so I laughed along.

That was pretty much our conversation after two years of not seeing one another. Right before we parted ways, she grabbed my hand and asked if I'm married yet. I think that question was her way of extending our conversation. I told her no. I told her that she would the first to know and that she would have to attend the wedding. "My little brother is too good-looking to not be married," she said as she held onto my hand. She would always find a way to get in the last word. After all these years and all this questioning, I still won't tell her that I'm gay. Not that she would care, I'm pretty sure. I'm just afraid that she would stop asking if she knew. And I don't want our conversation to ever end.

On retaining my sense of humor

I was sitting in a café in Brooklyn reading Thich Nhat Hanh's *How to Sit*. This was his first in a series of books on mindfulness. I was sitting at a table in a row of tables. A woman at the next table was but a few feet in distance from my right. She was wearing headphones. She was eating her lunch, a pressed sandwich. I knew this because this was all they served in that café. She was listening to something. Occasionally, she would speak up, or was she speaking out of context and into that space? She was unaware that I was there, a short distance to her right. I have a way of being invisible in certain parts of the world, Bushwick, Brooklyn being one of those parts. No. Fuck that. This was my world as much as it was hers. Still, I was invisible, so much so that she was passing gas and was unaware of her own body or mine in proximity or perhaps she didn't care. I've already made my point, but this needed repeating.

So there I was, confronted with a question. Once conceiving it, I will carry this question with me always. I will ask it at dinner parties. I will survey my friends and family alike. Over time I will develop a more refined way of posing such an inquiry. For now, I asked this of myself. Do I confront this person? I was trying to be civil. She was white and I am not. I was not going to make this about race. Who was I kidding here? How I move through the world and take up space will always be about race. So, do I move and relocate? That was always the solution for the immigrant other in every neighborhood our family lived in. I've been in this country for 47 fucking years. Did I just refer to myself as an immigrant yet again? I did move down that row that day. But before doing so, I conjured up a rebuttal in the hopes of reminding her of my presence and her sense of being present. Her sense of smell, her sense of hearing. I farted loud and with purpose. I scented her a message, as if to say, "Oh, hi, and how are you today?" Her contorted look of utter disgust, I'll remember with a smile. If not, these words will bring me back. As we locked eyes, as we looked intently at one another, I wanted to believe that we saw ourselves as neighbors in that moment, in between.

On being shaped by the deeds of others

Had I not said what I had said. Had I said, "Thank you for your consideration of my application, thank you for your show of support, for your commitment to diversity, for your willingness to be my colleague." Had I not said, "Please don't talk to me about diversity, about this coming down to a close and competitive race." Had I not said, "Let's not forget that you just hired the husband of the chair and he is white." Had I not said that in that moment, maybe by now I would be a tenured professor. Maybe my life as a tenured professor would be too busy protecting my class standing, my place as someone inside to be an artist out here, and I would never have written the book I did. Maybe there would have been nothing to write about.

Then again, maybe I could write something imagined, something I want to write about. Had I just nodded and played along, as was expected of my Brown presence. Had I enacted what I was taught, the presence of absence, this work of silence. Had I just said, "Thank you for this." Or "Thank you for that." Had I just said, "Thank you for everything and anything, for the gesture of being my colleague, for calling me professor. I should have known better. You meant it as a joke." Had I laughed along when really you wanted to say, "Clean up on aisle 4." Had I known my place and played the part, perhaps there would be no story to tell, no facts to document, no book written to trigger your response of wanting it erased. No claims of defamation of the other. Perhaps I would be telling the story of a Brown body in academia who overcame the odds, who is again playing the part and is now among those to be tolerated as other. The question is, who gets to, who wants to claim this identity of the other? Is it the white man who claimed the first job? Never mind that he was married to the department's chair. Never mind that he was hired by a committee consisting of three white persons. I would say "white people" but even I am uncomfortable with how it sounds in this sentence, two of whom were tenure-track professors still beholden to the department chair's written endorsement to gain the status of having tenure. If this is too much to hold or process, then let's just stick with the original wording, a committee of three white people.

Or is it the other white man claiming his innocence in claiming yet another job. Does he get to claim that he is being defamed because I have written the book, that I am writing this essay? Is it defamation when the facts are clearly stated, as clear as can be when convoluted by whiteness. Again, this needs to be stated for legal purposes, that the white man was not given but selected, recommended, chosen for a job, that the white man holds a bachelor's degree in an entirely different field and that he was hired to be a professor in a creative writing department. And hired by a committee of three white people. Imagine a world where someone Brown or someone Black can claim that kind of privilege or . . . I won't even bother finishing that thought. I am incapable of processing such a privilege. Had I not been disqualified or, as they claimed, had my application not been removed from consideration due to not meeting the criteria of the written job ad. And, again, I state, had none of this happened. Had I not been a Brown man. This thought occurs to me every so often, perhaps when something like this happens and it is bound to happen again and again. Conditioned as it were, I am still overwhelmed with thoughts of shame. I wonder if white people have similar thoughts.

If this seems obsessive, it is because I am obsessed with moving on. I am trying to write another book about another subject in a form that is not poetry. Even when I am being honored with an award for a book I've written about experiences I never wanted and yet endured, I am reminded. I am always reminded of that place and of my place. I keep putting it down and it keeps coming back, this weight that I carry of someone else's shame.

Had this not happened. Had I not said what I said back in that moment, would I be saying this now? "Thank you for the honor of the American Book Award. This is a book that I did not want to write. This is the book that I had to write. Do I wish that the lived experience of this book was not endured? Yes. Am I proud of this book? Yes. Why? Because I have written myself out of silence and back into existence. Had I not said, had I not done, this version of myself would not exist. So to all of you who made this happen"—I am referring to you and you and you and you—"thank you for everything you did to me." And that part about having said or having not said, let me write this as the addendum: "Thank you. You did this. You all did this. Go fuck yourself. And again, thank you."

On the aftermath

I am always open to engaging in conversations. I've learned from years of a legal struggle that I am not in any position to initiate dialogue and, if I do, it needs to be documented and in public. I cannot communicate by way of backchannels for fear that it will be scrutinized by the white people who would want to do me harm. I do have it within me to respond. I will do so with honesty, openness, a conveyance of my perspective, and a willingness to listen. To all those who have contributed to the much-needed conversation, thank you. I will stay true to my commitment to that book. I will not fight, defend, or perform my otherness to those I consider to be members of my community. I will instead address the lurkers, the watchers, and those who would anticipate, and even celebrate, the tensions between Brown and Black people. That book, this book, this moment, is about white. It was always about white. I will not lose focus. I state these words yet again.

I wrote a book. I presented the facts. I wrote a book that is about my experiences, about what happened to me. If you are questioning the who, where, and when in what I've written, my wounds are not a timeline. They are not linear or mapped for you to prove or disprove. If you have questions about inclusivity or exclusion, if you are thinking that this is in any way diminishing you or your contributions, know that when I wrote that book, I took great care and consideration for who is named in a book written without names and who is inside and whom I care to not include. If you see yourself in this book, it is because you have been implicated. If you are wondering why you have not been acknowledged, why you were left out, I want you to know that this is not about exclusion. It is about respect and concern. I will not conflate one race with another. I will not pit my being, my image, my struggles against that of another. To do so would be diminishing to both you and me. To posit my perspective as to how we as Brown and Black bodies function and exist in the convoluted workings of whiteness would be disrespectful in the book, this statement. Your accomplishments are yours and no one can take that from you. Not the white people with their elaborate maneuverings to uphold whiteness, or me with claims of knowing what they did to you or me, not that I would claim to know your struggles. If you should see yourself at this moment, know that I am here. I am speaking to you. I am open. I will gladly speak with you. I will respect your privacy, your presence, your autonomy. If you are asking for my story, I will tell you my story. I'm just not that interested in your version of my story. I will continue to state the facts. I will continue to speak my truth. About that book. That book is about what happened to me. Whiteness was and is inflicted. This is about what is still happening to me.

On considering what this is not about

If I cannot say what this is about, let me say what this is not. This is not a story about a six-year-old boy who is being accused of racism. Or that of a boy who experienced or is claiming his experience of racism as a six-year-old boy. Or that of my present self as a 57-year-old Asian man. Perhaps now I can say what I know to be true. This is about feeling and knowing something in the body, that even at the age of six, I felt something that told me that I was different. It took some years but as soon as I found the language, a way, the audacity to say it, I said I was gay. The other thing that happened that day, I felt it in the body. I felt it being made into a memory. I felt it being tucked away beneath layers of skin, tissue, muscles developing and dissipating with time, a memory waiting for when I would find the words to say. This is about knowing my otherness. This otherness exists in proximity to race. This story, this body, this memory, this knowing. The otherness that shows itself as pride, as defiance, otherness as seen in a mother who does not speak the language, in the excitement of being invited, in both your mother and you, otherness as a lie you told as a six-year-old, you told this lie to your mother to shield her from what? You did not know and now you know. This otherness of saying while looking forward or looking back, this lens of race, I have no way of turning it off. This memory that I am calling "otherness," I've kept it with me for all these years.

On Teaching

On considering career suicide

When the person reached out to me prior to the publication of my previous book, he said that he was worried. That what I was doing would amount to career suicide. Truth be told, I had no words for him in that moment. I wrote about it in the book but even then, I had only the wherewithal to ask a simple question consisting of one word: why? A question I was asking of myself. I thought I would ask it of this person in the hopes that he could shift. Did he? In past articulations of this very subject, I referred to the person as a colleague. I refrain from such a term now. I've come to realize that language makes it possible to lie to oneself. I've had some time to think since that book's release to learn the work of unlearning.

Perhaps now I can attempt to answer in earnest and in truth. We are not colleagues. You express concern as someone white, someone tenured, and someone with a career. I am none of the above. I am Brown. I have jobs teaching. I have a mortgage. It's something of a miracle that I can make this monthly mortgage. I have since lost one of my teaching jobs because of the book I published about academia. I did this knowingly, but with some trepidation because I did heed your warnings.

But is this suicide? I am breathing again. I found a way to write this response. I feel resolute in saying we are not colleagues. I have not heard from you since that time. Then what are we? I will refrain from answering my question.

On the expectations of giving it away

It happens. We as writers, more specifically, as poets, spend so much of our lives writing that book. For some of us, it might be our only book. It is our everything, if not for our lifetime, at least for a period of our lives. It is a source of great pride and something that we want so badly to share with the world.

I see this as a teacher of poetry. I see this in my students who spend countless hours and crucial resources to get that first book into print. A friend from childhood whom I do not communicate with very often, called me out of the blue the other day. He asked how I was doing. I said, "Alive." That is my stock answer at this time. He then asked what I'd been doing. I said that I write, that I've been writing books of poetry. He was surprised and genuinely curious. I found out that he worked with computers for a living. He lamented the drudgery of this occupation. I found out that he not only worked with computers, he designs them and I too was genuinely curious. As we ended our conversation, he said, "Send me a book; I want to tell my kids that you write." I said, "OK." I said this out of the habit of wanting to be seen, of having been seen at that moment in exchange. I think my friend is a genuinely nice guy. I think he meant well but I also think he is conditioned by a society that sees the work I do as a writer as something of a conversation to be had over dinner. If I send the book, I am sure he would share my work with his kids. Perhaps he would even read out loud a poem or two and encourage his kids to try writing poetry. I said I would send it and so I will. I should have said, "Send me a computer, so that I can tell my students what people are doing as we sit here writing poetry." I am writing this to you specifically as poets. I am writing this as a way of reminding myself. This is my work, our work. This is my worth, our worth.

On a question and the answer that followed

I gave a lecture over Zoom to a group of high school students in Skokie, Illinois. I did my usual routine of poetry reading, talking craft, holding space, and pausing to emphasize meanings. I answered questions born of assignments, the big questions that teenagers ask about being poets. How do you know when the poem is finished? How do you write what really matters? I do this work with the students in mind, their hopes of belonging, their desires to say what they have yet to find the words to say. In this way, I thought I was doing what I was supposed to be doing.

I've written about teaching before but never for the purpose of learning for myself. This was the question from afar by a teenager on a screen. I remember the awkwardness of her movement, how she walked up to the microphone, removed her mask, hesitated, then asked, "Are you OK?"

Are you OK? A simple enough question asked by a child. It took a minute before I knew how to respond, "I'm OK. Can I ask why you asked me that just now?" She shrugged her shoulders. She said, "I read your book. Sometimes we just need someone to ask."

On the English Language

I am undeniably sentimental in what I've been writing as of late. But the unabashed truth is, I have been sentimental with words all my English-speaking life. That is because I have been made to believe that the English language is something to be in awe of. It is the language of Shakespeare and the Queen, somebody's queen somewhere. It is the lyrics to rock and roll and a Declaration of Independence written by those who would pen the act of enslaving another into law. Wait, why am I in awe of this language? Because I was told at a very young age that I was good at this English language thing. Because of how I talked, my teacher told me to be a politician. I took it as a compliment, until I paused and thought about it. I then took her comment as an insult. In English, I thought, but did not say, "Go fuck yourself, lady."

When asked, I tell my Vietnamese relatives that I teach poetry at a college, and the immediate reaction in the room is to say something about being smart. They are not really talking about me. They are talking about the English language. My cousin, in English, changes the subject. He's interested in stock options and friends-and-family discounted buy-in rates. I escape into the next room, where a Korean soap opera is playing on TV. Monotone and out of sync, it too has been dubbed into the English language.

On reading as a way of looking, seeing

It occurred to me that even as I am writing a book on art and writing, I have referred to very few writers. Perhaps now is as good a time as any to come clean about this little-known fact: I do not like reading. Well, it's not that I don't like reading; it's just that I am not a good reader. Nothing I read in school ever made any sense. History, science, those things in math they refer to as word problems—I called them word salads, words mixed up and made indigestible, incomprehensible. Throughout school, reading was an act of regurgitation. I threw up this language without ever being fed. I resorted to the desperate act of memorization. It kept me from failing, but I barely passed.

This began as an essay about dyslexia. I thought I was going to do my part to shed some light on a condition that many of us live with. I have lived with it my entire life. I've written thus far in an effort to arrive at a declaration. I don't like reading. I'm not a good reader. I was going to take that as a position and claim my love of writing and the imagination, that thing we often do of taking the bad and making it good, forcing a circle into a square. That concept won't make it to the finish line on this go-round. The subject is too important to me and, as such, I still need to find a way to write about it with clarity. What I am clear on for now is that I do not have it in me to write about the subject just yet. Maybe by the time I arrive at an ending for this book I will. There are still things in the way. This notion of not liking to read felt false even as I was writing it down.

I spent a lot of time in libraries, like many poor immigrant kids growing up. Our mothers discovered a not-so-well-kept secret. It was that librarians were babysitters free of charge. They didn't ask questions. Several days a week, during the school year, I would be instructed by my mother to go to the library while on my way home. Stay at the library. Do not come home until it closes, or before it gets dark, depending on the season or whether she was offered overtime. I was instructed to do my homework and then read a book. Instead, I spent my afternoons looking at pictures. I had a penchant for home decor, cookbooks, and cars. They were the wholesome dreams of a hungry 12-year-old.

This was true to a certain extent. But who am I kidding here? I spent a lot of time looking for images of naked men, in books and magazines, and on the covers of romance novels. Anatomy books, sex-ed books, physical health and bodybuilding magazines, Eadweard Muybridge's *Complete Human and Animal Locomotion*, and sometimes, if I was lucky, the pages inside *Cosmopolitan*. I spent my time looking and seeing, but rarely was I reading. Still, this is written about the act of reading. It came by way of seeing first, specifically the cover of Anne Rampling's *Exit to Eden*. It was an illustration of a man's upper torso. He was presumably naked, with three crisscrossing lash marks on his lower back extending down towards his lower backside. I am trying to get the details of this right because I am trying to locate that very moment when I discovered my love of language.

Twelve years old and there I was, hiding in a corner of this library, in a reading nook with my head buried in a novel about sadomasochism. I hid the book jacket behind a column of other books. I devoured every word on every page. The book enthralled me. The book detailed an S&M relationship between a young man and an older woman, written in the alternating perspectives of a woman and her submissive. At 12, I read a book about a very adult subject meant to be read by other adults. I didn't understand all of its titillations, but I understood its implications. I discovered language's dirty little secret. It told me I was gay, again and again, and I loved it for that very reason.

I read and reread, each time knowing a little more. For months and years, I kept returning to that library to read the dog-eared pages of my favorite parts. There were many. I finally found the courage one day, somewhere in my teenage years, to bring the book to the checkout counter. I slid the book with its Brodart-covered jacket to the attending librarian. She looked at the cover. She made a comment about it looking like an interesting read, and then she stamped it with a return date, no questions asked.

This is not quite what I had hoped for. I set out to write about dyslexia. It'll happen one day. For now, I've written all this just to arrive at saying this: I do like reading but I'm still not a good reader. And the writer of that book was better known as Anne Rice. Yes, the same Anne Rice who wrote about vampires and New Orleans and covens of witches also wrote about Elliot, the submissive, who was my first and only literary crush.

On counting cranes

(A LIFELONG COLLABORATION OF ART, FRIENDSHIP, AND FAMILY)

A student came to me long ago with what I thought was a peculiar request. She asked that I allow her to fold cranes while attending my writing courses in the MFA program in Poetry. She said it helped her with her anxiety. I said, "Yes." Even though I thought it strange at the time, I also found it endearing that she would be so forthcoming. She went on to take a number of my classes. We became connected, one Vietnamese to another. She had this habit of arriving late, shouldering a minimum of three tote bags, coffee in one hand, some canned sweetened iced tea in the other. When she walked into a room, time had a way of standing still—that is, until she found her seat, positioned her belongings, and began the rhythms of her folding. One day at the beginning of the semester, she came in late. I remember saying, "Ho, what am I going to do with you?" I also remember the collective gasp that swept over the room and the awkward silence that followed. What was I thinking? Did I really just say that? A pocket of laughter from those who knew her came from one side of the room and then another and then another. She said, "Hi, everyone, I'm Carolyn Ho." I have been trying to tell this story in all the ways it was so wrong and still with some amount of saving grace, because I believe this story will forever be the thing that binds us. It was an epic moment of awkwardness between two Vietnamese people caught in the lost and found of our lives in translation.

Carolyn Ho eventually graduated from the program. Sometime later, she arrived at my front door with a garbage bag full of folded cranes. I have been counting them ever since the delivery of that first bag: 132,402 cranes and counting. I am now the godfather of her son Tai. She continues to fold cranes and I continue to count. It has become a lasting commitment, a shared life, awkward and contentious at times, the family claimed at the lost and found. I've gone from being the curmudgeonly teacher to the curmudgeonly uncle, to godfather, to reluctant best friend, because you can't be both family and best friend, I'm saying this even now. But I also get to say without malice, hesitation, or hidden meaning whatsoever, "Ho, what am I going to do with you?"

On being taught by my student

I have this habit of demurring at my existence. I preface myself by saying that I am not as angry as people perceive me to be. I say this as it relates to my writing and often in my presentation of the work. I say this, and it is often met with a kind of acceptance, even sighs of relief, from the other. In those moments, I've invoked a clause that says our friendship or relation can remain intact in the aftermath of reading *Book of the Other*. I was saying this to my student the other day. She said she read my book, and before she could finish what she was saying, I said that I am not as angry as the book made me out to be, as though some part of me was saying I was not the one who wrote the book. Why did I feel the need to interject in that moment? Why this condition of having to apologize, of having to deny this register of anger? What my student said to me in that moment in response, I will keep with me always. "But you are angry, Truong, and you have every right to be angry. I read your book and I am angry for you. I didn't live what you had to live through and still, I'm angry for what they did to you. For what they are doing to me as a student in that place, for what this world is capable of doing." And then she said, "You need to be angry. You get to be angry." As a teacher, I'm always learning from my students.

On the other's reflection

At the dinner table, my five-year-old godson wanted in on the adult conversation. He said, "Don't be a pussy, Truong." And just like that, the room fell silent. After being questioned and receiving a makeshift lecture on the misogyny of a word, the child proceeded to shift tones; awakened to his own awareness, he found a way to walk back his language. The word became *puss*, then *push*, then *pushy*, and the blame squarely landed on the shoulders of some unnamed teacher.

Yes, the word was *pushy*, or so the child would have us believe. And I wanted to believe. I wanted that momentary relief of not having to prepare my godson for the fallacy that is the English language. I wanted to preserve his sense of discovery. I want to believe that words are tools as much as they are weapons. This is what I want to teach my godson, but slowly, over time. And when the English language fails, and it will fail, I want my godson to have another means of saying what he believes, to know that a word, like a brick, can build or break. I want to save the warnings for later, for when he'll know when to reject such warnings.

⊙

In my first semester of graduate school, 29 years ago, I took a class titled The Work of Silence. It was taught by a woman, an Asian woman. I will not name this person out of my deep respect for and desire to protect her—not that she needs protecting. She was and is profoundly brilliant to me. The class forever shaped me as a writer and even more importantly, it changed me as a human being.

It introduced me to the work of Edmond Jabès, Lorine Niedecker, Stéphane Mallarmé, Maurice Blanchot, and Paul Celan. They wrote from the perspective of isolation, loss, and exile. This was the work that came after the disaster. How does one write in the language of one's destroyer? As a Vietnamese refugee writing in the English language, I connected with these writers and their positions at the margins. I remember thinking about my classmates, all of whom were white except for one other poet, speaking in a language about languages, all of which were not my own. I remember my pride in being taught by this professor, a poet and a scholar who so clearly embodied her consciousness and perspective as a person of color. I remember witnessing her presence as a professor, her rigorous inquiry as a scholar, and thinking that this is what it means to be empowered, to be seen for your work, and to be doing this work as a person of color. This notion of authority, this realization of the conflict festering deep inside myself, did not surface until I too became a teacher in the space of the academy. How was I to navigate the teaching and inquiry of a craft and a field that was and still is so predominantly white? As a graduate student, I remember thinking that things will change because they must, that people like my professor would pave the way. How is it then that I, as a teacher, still find myself entrenched within this culture of invisibility and silence?

As I write this now, I cannot remember reading a single poet in that graduate course that allowed me a connection in terms of my identity. I was impressed, perplexed, and bewildered by the language. I was conflicted with the conversations I encountered on the page. Many of these books were originally written in languages I did not understand and then translated into the English language, which I still did not understand. At the time, I did not see this as a problem but rather as a point of intellectual inquiry. In fact, I remember thinking that for once in my life, I was not limited to the experiences of my identity. I loved the fact that, for the first time, I was being taught poetry by a person of color, by an Asian poet, by someone I very much identified with. I was no longer limited to the poetics of my skin.

It was as though I found a box full of lost keys in a stall at the flea market. I had these keys. I kept them in my pockets, and I obsessively threaded these keys through the various locks that kept me on the other side of knowing. And even when I could not gain access, I had these keys. I would show them as proof that I belonged, if not inside, then somewhere within proximity. If I could just find the right key, I could open that door to the endless possibilities of language.

This instructor called me *kiddo*. That will always stay with me. She asked me questions and sometimes she would even show signs of frustration that I wasn't getting something I needed to get. I was not saying what needed to be said. She taught as though what she shared with me was not just about poetry, but rather about life, about survival. There was an urgency in her voice. I will always remember her saying something to the effect of "Be careful of the stage, the one you are building, because once built, you will find yourself performing on it." I admit that during those times of being in her presence, I did not understand some of what was being said. I pretended to know. I struggled to find something to say. I wanted her to know that I was present. I still want her to know that I am present, and I am still trying to find that key that will allow me to say what needs to be said.

Even as I am writing this now, I am afraid of what it means to question what came before. I am afraid of conveying any notions of doubt in the teachings of my professor. I would not be a writer today had it not been for her teachings 29 years ago. Even more importantly, I would not be a teacher.

And still, my internal conflict with this material and the avant-garde nature of experimental poetics served to isolate me as a person of color in the whiteness of that world. I write this from my perspective as a writer, a student, and now a teacher. I can only imagine the challenges of teaching such a subject from the perspective of my teacher. It was 1992 and a different world, or so I wanted to believe.

◉

When I was seven, I learned that language was a conduit. Coupled with my curiosity, I wielded this newfound power. I was my mother's helper in her business as a seamstress. She was known as the Vietnamese woman who could sew just about anything. Her reputation grew as they came from all over the neighborhood and beyond. She made dresses and curtains and dresses out of curtains. She made little girl dresses and mother dresses and sexy woman dresses, all while not speaking a single word of

English. With women, my mother found a way of communicating with fabrics, buttons, colors, and all things pretty and beautiful. My mother had a language of her own.

My mother also had a number of male customers, mostly awkward young white boys who were sent to our house by their mothers or came of their own accord. These boys on the verge of becoming men would come to my mother in search of the white suit with flare-bottom slacks. It was the year of John Travolta and "Stayin' Alive." My mother was determined to not only stay alive but to thrive, and she was known for making the best-fitting suits in various shades of white. Unlike her interactions with the women, and for reasons I did not understand as a child, she would not speak directly to these boys. As such, I was my mother's translator in all things related to these young white boys, who would grow up to become white men. In this way, I learned about power at a young age.

On one occasion, a boy, around 17, came to the house. He was hesitant and nervous. He arrived as though he had been tasked with this responsibility. He spoke politely of the specifics of this suit to be made, knowing that his manners would be received by the older woman, my mother. As the translator to both this boy and my mother, I held authority over both parties at that moment. He spoke as if speaking through me and I diligently translated his every word. My mother in return responded with succinct instructions that included the removal of his coat so that measurements could be made. I translated, instructed, and asserted by way of intonations. But as an opportunistic seven-year-old gay boy—although "gay" was not yet part of my vocabulary—I told the boy to go to the bathroom across the hall and take off all his clothes so that accurate measurements could be made. I said, with authority, "My mother wants you to . . ." The boy did as he was told, though hesitantly. He took his time. I remember my mother being concerned. She asked why he was in the bathroom and why it was taking him so long. She told me to knock on the door and tell him to hurry up. Again, I chose my words carefully, "My mother says you need to come out." My mother and I waited for another minute. We heard the bathroom door open. The boy walked out, shy and awkward, having followed my instructions. The boy was naked.

My mother let out a scream that quickly turned into yelling in a language that the naked teenager did not understand. But still, he knew enough to retreat into the bathroom and put on his clothes. He tried to apologize. My mother wanted him to go, and so I said, "My mother wants you to leave." He left and never returned. For the rest of the day, I heard my mother mumbling this and that about Americans and this place and white boys and their ways.

I've been trying to write this for most of my adult life. I've tried writing it as a story of sexual awakening. I've tried to write about doors and keys and rooms located inside what I thought was my house. What is this notion of owning a house when you are seen as a guest in your own home? I've tried writing it as a story about the first time I discovered my love for teaching and the English language. I've tried to write it as a dark comedy, starring my immigrant mother as a beguiling presence in my plot to see a teenage boy naked for the very first time. I've tried writing this from the perspective of the shame I felt for having done this to my mother or the shame of the teenage boy who did what he was told. I wonder if I would recognize him today if I saw him in a room, fully clothed and existing as a white man in the world. Is he still doing what he's told?

My mother and I have never talked about what happened that day. My mother and I and this chasm of silence. Sometimes I laugh when retelling this story. I've learned to highlight humor. Sometimes I think about the shame. I think of my mother, and I think she knows. I think about the shame of not knowing a language, but also of the shame of knowing it all too well.

◉

I've spent the last 29 years enacting a work of silence in both my writing and the classroom as a teacher. I'd convinced myself of the power tucked inside of such a consciousness. I thought that writing in the code of abstract language allowed me to say what could not be said. I wrote books and hid my anger about injustices inside my books. I confronted my subject inside the book. Not understanding the code, various academics saw fit to invite me to their classes, to perform my otherness in their presence, naked in my words, the same way that teenage boy was naked in my mother's workroom. They did not see themselves in the work, nor did they truly see me.

I believed that silence could be enacted through the absence of language as a way of confronting and exposing racism. I believed that my silence was an act of protest. That silence was the key. I thought I had found the right key to unlock the door to the power of language. I opened what was once locked and I walked inside. Little did I know that I was walking into their house. I was a guest, playing by their rules. I was invited in, and then one day, the locks were changed, and I was locked out. On another occasion, the locks changed again, and I was locked inside, in silence. I would do this with my poetry and my teaching. I would do this in the academy, in my capacity as a teacher.

⊙

I tasked myself with writing an essay about learning and writing and teaching and language. Somewhere tucked inside all of this, I found a boy's exertion of power and a man's painful realization of the lack thereof. This is the hardest thing I've ever had to write, despite having just declared *Book of the Other* to be the hardest thing I'd ever written. In total, it took me 15 years to write that book and to say what needed to be said. I wrote about the reality of teaching others to write in the space of the academy, to hone their voices. Meanwhile, I, the teacher, was voiceless, fearful, existing in silence. I was living a lie.

As a teacher, I talked a good game about empowering oneself. I encouraged my students to claim their voices. As a cog in academia amongst my colleagues, I pretended to be empowered, when in reality, I existed, powerless. When I spoke up against what I saw as unfair practices, the hiring of a white spouse and white friends, or when I tried to contribute to the department's forced discourse about race and equitable representation, I was told to refrain from expressing my anger, frustration, and resentment. I was made unable to claim my own voice for having experienced what I understood to be discriminatory practices of an institution and a clear rendering of racism in the world. Moments of what I deemed to be courage and self-empowerment retreated into silence, and I existed within this culture of fear.

I wrote *Book of the Other* to break the silence, to move beyond this constant state of fear, of losing the one thing I love more than anything else, more than being an artist, writer, poet, or lecturer. I was afraid of losing my place and work as a teacher. For years, I stood in a room in front of my students, teaching the work of finding one's voice, writing into that voice, and claiming one's power as a writer. For years, I saw myself sitting in a corner of that room, witnessing my own work of silence and the silencing that was and is still being enacted by the institution. I am no longer willing to live this lie.

◉

What haunts you? What hunts you? What are you hunting? I was asked these questions by a student as a young teacher. And now I ask these questions to every student. These are teaching tools that extend beyond the classroom and into life. I tell my students that if they commit to the answers, engaging with the questions rigorously, they will have the necessary ingredients for a book. Each time I ask this of my students, I commit to answering these questions again. They have become the mason jars holding the excess of a life lived in silence.

I am haunted by this history of silence that convinces me that telling, speaking, and writing the truth is an act of bravery or courage. Why should something so human be made so rare and labeled as such? Salman Rushdie was stabbed 15 times as he was about to give a lecture on his writing. I am haunted by this news, and just like that, I am haunted by this answer to my question.

I am hunted by those who hide behind the moral code of the institution, who hide inside the color white, who seek to silence.

I am hunting for that thing that was taken from me. Perhaps *hunting* is not the right word after all. It implies capturing and killing. I have been captured and left to die a metaphorical death.

I am looking for my voice in an effort to live, exist, and speak the truth. This is the hardest thing I've ever written.

Perhaps now is when I make note of these facts: I am a teacher in the academy. I am a lecturer. I am not a professor. My presence in the academy is that of a laborer, that of a layperson, that of one who is silent for having been silenced in the academy. I did not write this to entertain. I wrote this for my teacher. I am not performing my otherness. If you think that this is funny—the naked teenager, the work of silence rendered as a silent movie, my godson and the word, my name—then what's written is funny, but not by choice. If you are asking for more, well, that's not funny. I say this now. I posit this here. This is my refusal to remain unnamed, to laugh along. This is pertinent to the consciousness of this essay, the labor I'm doing. My name is Truong Tran.

On Imagination and Memory

On the boy who was my first love

In the fourth grade, I met a boy who climbed to the highest point of the tallest log that was planted erect in the neighborhood playground. It must have been at least 20 feet high and about a foot in diameter. There was no reason why it existed on that playground; perhaps it was a remnant of what was there before. To the boys in the neighborhood, it was a source of great inspiration. To climb that log and claim it as your conquest was a dream to many, but few dared to attempt such a perilous feat. There were grooves notched in it and protruding bumps of wood that added to the temptation. This resulted in a number of broken arms and legs, but no one died, to the best of my knowledge.

He did it on a day when there was no one there to witness his triumph, no one, that is, but me. We were not yet friends at the time of his climb. I was trying to make it across the monkey bars, something that I'd never been able to do. Halfway through, I lost my grip and fell to the ground. I looked up and saw this boy clawing his way up this log of wood. He not only made it to the top but found a way to get himself into an upright position. He stood there precariously balanced with his back to the sun as he proceeded to urinate on the world below. I remember looking up, seeing the silhouette of this boy in the sky, his body outlined by the sun from behind. It was as if god had appeared and this was his sentence onto the world: a shimmering stream of gold arching its way to the ground below. I was nowhere near its descending path, yet I felt the need to seek shelter from his wrath.

He made his way down as I watched from a distance with trepidation. He came over to where I was. He said, "You saw that, didn't you? You saw what I did." He said, "I'm Tuong." And I said, "I'm Truong." Our names were only a letter apart, but our lives then and now couldn't be more different. That day, I made a friend. I said, "I saw," and as such, a moment became a memory held. There is so much more here that wants to be told. For now, let this be the story of how I saw a boy do the impossible. Let this be a promise fulfilled of witnessing another's triumph. It happened. I saw what he did. It matters that I am saying this, even now.

I want to write this as a remarkable story even if it ends on a note of heartache, as is the case of most stories of first love, of the unrequited kind. A story that begins with a boy still learning to be himself, to be gay, and a boy who is clearly not gay. What happened, what shaped, what was shared, and what was left unspoken all these years should be enough to make this story a story worth telling.

On the creek that cuts across Singleton Road

There is something about the place that just resists the telling of a story. There, memories are tucked deep within my consciousness, fragments and shards that promise to cut. How is it that such an insignificant patch of dirt and some water, in terms of its geography, can be so magical and cruel and haunting and divisive all at once?

I tried going back there the other day. I say this as though I was just there last month, when, in reality, the last time I rode the school bus across that narrow road, I was in the seventh grade. I was 13 years old. I asked a friend to drive me there in the hopes that she could drive me through. We both lived in the neighborhood as kids. She couldn't understand my obsession with that place. I wanted to know this for myself.

It was nothing like I had remembered it in my youth. There was no longer a dip in the road or water that ran and pooled on either side of that two-lane path. There were no trees, no semblance of nature holding on for dear life. There were no bicycles abandoned at the water's edge, left to corrode into the soil. There was no island made of rubber tires and shopping carts, no place for refuge from a father's wrath or was it a refuge for a father's love? And, perhaps the saddest of my recent observations, there was no path through, no escape for both the *haves* and the *have-nots*. There was no road for that matter. No water, no evidence of my past.

There is something in the language of this rendering that is trying to make the place beautiful, these memories that refuse to be. Why do I need to write this with beauty? Why this need to see it so?

I caught crawdads in that creek. I kept one as a pet. It lasted only days in a plastic tub sprinkled with dirt from where it came from. It sat in the sun. I learned about death long before I learned how to live. One afternoon, my brother and I caught a bag full. I asked my mother if we could eat them. She melted some butter. She boiled them in water. When cooked, they made the house smell like a mechanic's shop. My mother threw them out and told us to never swim in that dirty water. I learned how to climb trees back in those days, back at that creek. Each time I climbed, I climbed a bit higher until I learned that I could hide. I didn't know then that hiding was a way of witnessing the world.

There, hidden in that tree, I saw a teenage boy I knew from the neighborhood, being beaten by his father. The teenager was a child hiding inside a burgeoning man's body. We didn't hang out or anything like that. He was too old to be my friend, but he was kind in our interactions. He said "Hi" on occasion and once even told his kid brother to shut up when the kid made some joke about chinky this or chinky that. He was ordered to find a branch, "a good one," his father said. He was ordered to lower his pants and bare his backside, in the familiar ritual between fathers and sons. He was looking around. He saw me hiding in that tree. He said nothing. He was pleading with his father and then he did as he was told. He handed his father this weapon of his own choosing to be used for his own punishment. I was a child myself witnessing this act of a father's cruelty, or was it love, and why did it have to happen in that public yet presumably private space, there in that creek? Perhaps there was a lesson to be learned about the transference of shame from the father to the son to the witness perched above. I wanted to know that teenager's offense, the father's resolve, and my arousal as I witnessed it happening from a distance. He cried, but barely. Even as he was being punished in public, he knew well enough to keep a secret and to meet the expectation of taking it like a man.

I saw a girl kissing a boy. I saw her curiosity as my own. And then I saw her wanting to change her mind, to stop a moment that would become a lifetime. I saw her resist, struggle, cry, hit, and then get hit. I saw the surrendering in her body, the muscle giving up and going limp. I saw her looking away from her own story, staring off into a distant something or maybe nothing. This all happened in a matter of minutes. I heard my own silence. I saw them walking away. He held her hand as he walked ahead. He dragged her down that dip in the path. From my vantage point up in that tree, I saw them emerge on the other side. Those minutes of witnessing, how was I to know, in the instance of it happening, that I would be carrying this weight equivalent to a lifetime of knowing?

There are stories that will always resist the act of being told. There are details within that remain out of context, deliberately so. That time on the school bus while crossing the creek on that narrow two-lane road, a girl in the back started screaming. She said she saw a dead body in the water. The bus driver didn't stop. It was important, I guess, to stay on schedule. That night, the local news confirmed the girl's claim. My parents and those of the other kids in the neighborhood forbade us from going down to that creek ever again.

Not long after that last news report, maybe months, a year at best, our family moved to another corner of the same town, yet another *have-not* neighborhood full of immigrant aspirations, still prone to the allure of ice cream truck music, but inching closer to the neighborhood of *the haves*, to the homes of those whose children had the privilege of swimming and drowning in their own backyards. There was no dip on any road in this new neighborhood, no creek to discard one's oil change from a hand-me-down Ford Pinto. There was no tree tall enough to climb, to hide. There was no vantage point to take on the burden, curiosity, or titillation of witnessing. But bodies still had a way of showing up. They were dumped, still breathing, in vast fields of newly cleared orchards.

On queerness and the imagination

From high up in a tree, I sat and saw a father beat his nearly grown son with a switch. I was moved by the fear of being discovered and aroused by the excitement of being a witness to the ritualized enactment of a contract inked in masculinity; the submission of the son and the assertions of the father all played out in this theater of cruelty.

I felt a desire in the minutes that followed to console the boy as a boy. To salve his bruised and welted skin, to feel his heaving body as he sobbed with his head pressed against my chest, cradled in my arms. I was barely in my teens and he was just shy of being an adult. I wanted to imagine this care and comfort between a white teenager who would grow up to be a white man and an Asian immigrant boy who would grow up to become distrustful of white men.

He saw me in the tree but remained silent at that moment. As such, I was made a witness to his shame and suffering, a teenager on the cusp of becoming a man being bared and beaten as a boy. From where I sat up in that tree, I could hear his muffled grunts of defiance that became the breathless gasps of anguish that became the cries of a boy wanting desperately to be a man. I can still hear the progression of our movement through sound, of his regression from the edge of manhood back into the brokenness of youth. The sound of that switch cutting through the air, striking his backside, each stroke growing louder with the insistent marking of a father's will. I heard the father saying, "I'll beat it out of you if that's what it takes." Between the boy's cries and the father's thundering voice, I heard, "I'm sorry. I'm sorry." But these were not said as apologies. "I'm sorry." They were pleas of a boy for a father's love. Why do I insist on rendering this as love?

I added to this symphony with the synchronized pace of my own heartbeat. I heard it getting louder to the extent that I was afraid of it making its way out of my body and into the world. I was afraid that it would say what I could not. In my own journey in that moment of witnessing, I went from curiosity to the peak of excitement, to unknowing arousal, to dread then fear for a boy I wanted to know and wanted to save. I wanted to say, "Stop. You're hurting him." But I too remained silent. I learned a lesson that day, that silence could become a condition of being. That evening, I masturbated to the memory of his faint cries.

I saw him in the weeks and months that followed. I watched him play touch football or stickball in the middle of our dead-end street. I would make the effort to find the ball that went astray, that would get lost in the weeds of my father's overgrown ground cover of ivy. I would hasten to find it just so that I could throw the ball back in his direction. Briefly in those moments of exchange, we would see and acknowledge one another. And—still this need to state the obvious—we never spoke about what happened.

I learned that his name was Shawn. (This was not his real name, but for the sake of this story, I needed a name. I needed to know that I did my part to keep some semblance of this silence. I needed a way to tell this story.) One of those times when I threw the ball in his direction, I said, "Hey, Shawn, catch." And to my surprise, he said,

"Thanks, bro." He paused for a brief second and then he asked, "Your name is Truong, right?" He called me "bro." In what little language we exchanged, something kind existed between us.

Years later and in my twenties, I moved to San Francisco. I came out as gay. I found a place, my community, and a sense of belonging. I was attending a wedding reception one evening when I saw this same teenage boy arriving as a man. We sat across from one another at a banquet-style dinner table. I reintroduced myself, saying, "I once knew a boy named Shawn. Your name . . ." and before I was able to finish my sentence, he said, "And I knew a boy named Truong." There was a moment shared of honest elation. It was as though we were childhood best friends who had found each other as adults. The moment subsided and the familiar awkwardness came flooding back. We tried. I really believe that we tried our best. We spoke that evening between the gaps of lingering silence. We exchanged memories of our versions of that town, of the street we lived on, and of that creek. We started talking about that creek and the trees and then we stopped. We just came to a halting stop.

It was as though we both decided, in that instant, to back away from what was being excavated. I remember thinking about how was it that we lived in the same neighborhood, on the same street within proximity to one another, and still we had such different experiences of our shared world. Perhaps the only thing that was really shared was the memory of that day, of what I saw, what he endured, and what he allowed me to witness by remaining silent. Why did he not tell his father that there was a boy sitting in a tree, watching, intently watching? Was that his way of protecting me? Was he ashamed? Was he inviting me in to witness his shame? Why am I writing this now? Why put into words the very thing that wants to be silent? This intimacy of what we shared happened in between the act of witnessing and being witnessed. What we shared, was it enough, was it too much? Was I an accidental witness to yet another white man's shame? And whose shame have I been carrying for all these years? His or mine or that of the father, whose name I never felt the need to know? Why was this held as a memory of queerness, and why this cruelty of the imagination?

We exchanged numbers when the time arrived for awkward goodbyes. It was not as if we ever said hello. I wanted to tell him that I was gay. Some part of me wanted to believe that we were old friends, that we would find a way to reconnect and stay connected. I wanted to know if he was gay. I think I knew, but I wanted the intimacy that comes with asking. We said we would call but made a point to not make promises. What would we have talked about in a coffee shop or over dinner in a place far away from that place? We never did. Again, this need to state the obvious. We never talked about what happened.

On the friendship that ended with a single phone call.

When I graduated with an MFA in Poetry, I was named the university's graduate hood recipient. That year, Hillary Clinton delivered the commencement speech. The college made a big deal about it. They painted the stadium a sniper-friendly color. They positioned the Secret Service both on stage and in the audience. As the hood recipient, I sat on stage in proximity to the First Lady, next to a middle-aged man who I was told was an agent in disguise. This is not a story about my graduation or the First Lady or the Secret Service, for that matter. I state this as a means of getting to the story that began only days after and all because I sat on that stage and made it onto the 10 o'clock news.

A columnist from the *San Jose Mercury News* caught wind of my presence on that stage from the news. She was Vietnamese, like myself. She must have thought that it would be a compelling story, a first-generation Vietnamese immigrant who would go on to become an American poet sitting on the same stage as the First Lady of the United States. The columnist's audience was the second-largest Vietnamese community in the U.S. I grew up in San Jose and my family planted roots there. It would make sense, I thought, my first outing as a looking-for-work poet. Little did I know, it would make the news for a different kind of outing.

The columnist arranged a meeting that ended up being a drawn-out phone conversation that, if I remember correctly, was contentious at times. It was our first and only conversation. She was bent on playing the part of the older sister. She wanted to frame the story of my life and how I arrived at this juncture, sharing the stage with Hillary Clinton. This was the story they wanted to hear and this was the story that she would give them. I wanted to talk about my writing, my love of language. As much as I tried, I could see my efforts were getting me nowhere. To add some spice to her preconceived perceptions of the hometown boy writing American poetry, she went deeper into the inquiry of my identity, in particular, into my love life, at least that which existed in my writing. She read my thesis or at least the parts that spoke of being gay. It was 1995 and I was only gay and out in certain places at certain times. My poetry happened to be one of those places. My hometown of San Jose was definitely not. She kept on probing as I kept on dodging until finally I said, "It's been too long and hard a road to get here as a writer to now make this about my gay identity. If it's OK with you, I would like to talk about my work as a writer." She quoted me verbatim and thus was my epic coming out story.

In hindsight, I could have said the statement made was off the record, but I didn't. It was definitely easier this way: one announcement in a newspaper that everyone and their grandmother read religiously. It was dignified and gave the illusion of being inadvertent. It was a single gesture rather than years of coming out at dinner parties, weddings, and family holiday gatherings. For the most part, people came to me with kind if misguided responses to this news. My mother cried and said she was worried about how the world will treat me. I said, "I don't care how the world is going to treat me. I only want to know how you're going to treat me." My sister said I couldn't be gay because I was nothing like our brother. She thought it was because I read too much. And so I came out yet again. I told her a secret. I didn't like reading.

And still this story is not about that time I sat on a stage with Hillary Clinton or the Vietnamese columnist who outed me in the *Mercury News* or how my mother or sister responded or how I outed myself as both gay and dyslexic to someone in my family for the first time. All this effort to arrive at a story. This is actually about a phone call someone made to me after the column came out in the news. He was one of my best friends all through high school. I answered the phone. I heard him say, "Tell me it's not true." I said, "It's true." I said, "Is that all you called me for?" He didn't respond. His silence in hindsight was loud and clear. I waited. Still no response. I said, "Goodbye." This was the story all along. In writing it, in reading this, I am not certain if it was even worth retelling and yet I've carried it all these years. Perhaps now I can finally put it down. I wrote this story not knowing why or how or where it would lead me. I did not think I would arrive at a question or a series of questions. I might as well ask it, in case you're reading. Why did the columnist care so much about the revelation of who I cared for or fucked or loved? Why did my high school friend take such great offense? Why did it matter? Why did he care? Why have I been carrying this for all these years? Twenty-eight years later, he's friends with me on social media, if not in real life. Do you still care? Because you called me with a question. You demanded a retraction of my very being. Again, the question: why hold on to this nothingness of a story? At least with this question, I can answer: as a way to put it down. I cared. I care. I'm human. I care that my being offended you so.

On racism and the imagination

There is so much to say here. So much that happened. So much still happening even now, yet I am compelled to make this short, direct, and to the point. There is a lifetime still to be endured. What is there left to imagine? A world erased of racism? Is this possible? Am I capable? Am I waiting still to be imagined? This is not one of those efforts to write the essay as a series of questions. There are assertions to be made. There are stories to be told. What happened to me in that particular place, in academia, I assert this here and now. That is racism. Call it what you will, favoritism, discrimination, nepotism as a non-triable offense, as the perfect defense to claiming one's privilege, whiteness. I say this in the present tense because racism when enacted will always be present. That I was falsely accused of stealing five dollars in a white woman's house in the fourth grade, that I am still writing about that now. Is this just a failure of the imagination? Yours or mine? In an imagined version of this story I could have been arrested, falsely accused, and put in juvie, and thus my failure to land the tenure-track job. Is this imagined if it happens in real life, all the time? Just ask a Brown or Black person. Imagine if they told you that racism is not real, that they earned everything, that in their version of the story, they earned the five dollars. They learned at a young age the values of hard work. They, as a Black woman or a Brown man, are the proof that racism does not exist in this place or that place. There is no need to imagine. This really happened. I'm sure it's happening even now.

On when imagination isn't needed

In the book that came before, *Book of the Other*, I wrote about my experiences as a teacher and more specifically what I experienced as a human being at the unrelenting hand of whiteness, at a university. I stated it then and I am stating it now. What I experienced was racism on an institutional and personal level that has forever changed my personhood. While it was happening, most people didn't know of its recurring enactment. I chose to remain silent because I liked my job. I loved my students. I was afraid of losing my connection to the world of teaching and writing. It was everything that I knew how to be. If being silent meant that I could continue to be a teacher and a writer, even if it meant that I accepted their treatment of me as a lesser human being, if it meant that I was doing both the work of teaching and writing in a state of silence, I would somehow find a way to do it. By silence, I am referring to that condition of existing in a lie. As it was happening to me in all the different ways I deemed to be racist, I did not respond. I did not speak up. I did not confront. I stood in front of my students and I talked about the power of writing and the power of their voices. I spoke the words, but they were not mine. They did not represent the reality of my existence. They were lies I told to sustain my livelihood as a teacher, to drown out the silence of my voice.

I did this work at that university for almost 20 years. I did it while playing by their rules. Over the course of those years, I kept on applying for tenure-track positions, only to be told that I was underqualified, or not the right composition of diversity, or removed from consideration because I did not meet the criteria of the written job ad, or that I'm loved by the department and by my students but sorry, not this time, or the next, or the next. I kept on applying with the hopes that something would change, that I would overcome racism in due time. I did all this while accepting the reality that a white man is still privileged with making a note in his evaluation of my interview for a better-paying job, a more equitable wage. That in his note, he stated without signing his name, "Truong is nice but small in comparison." I am assuming that the person I am being compared to was the one who got the job. That person was another white man who was given the position of being a tenure-track professor in an MFA program while only holding a bachelor's degree in another field. I stated this time and again as a fact, one of many facts of racism endured at the hands of whiteness. I thought that writing about my family's history, the stories of my childhood, the places I came from, my inability to read a book, or my discovery and curiosity of the naked male body at a young age, would somehow take me away from the inflection of race that defined my existence in this time. I thought that if I wrote this in a different form, away from the whiteness that calls itself poetry, I could create the distance needed to keep the racism of that place and of that world out of this book, but here it is and here I am writing about racism in the present tense. Once it happens, it keeps on happening.

Many of my former students who have read *Book of the Other* have been reaching out to offer support. They say they did not know. They say they are sorry. They say, "Fuck that place and fuck that department." They ask, "What can I do to support you in this time?" And I say, "Avenge me when I'm gone." I say this jokingly, as my mind is still fresh from writing about my childhood memories, of watching the kung fu flicks at the Jose Theater, where vengeance is the only way of existing. What then is vengeance in the context of my story? I tell my students to write in the face of all this fuckery, perhaps the truest form of vengeance: to take aim and assert your voice in the world; to question the social construct of a poem or a story; to insist that yours is a story worth telling, and to reject the silence that they've convinced you is your expression. I tell my former students that a lifetime of learning is a lifetime of being told where to hide and how best to hold your tongue, a lifetime of promises of when you will get to say your piece. Wait, they say. Wait for it. I tell my students, don't waste your time waiting for permissions, or invitations, or validations. Write. And write the fuck out of your writing.

At 57 years of age, I am following my own advice. I am only now writing about my dyslexia, a condition that's made me a master in the art of coping. Little did I know, my coping conditioned how I carried the weight of white people's ways.

On teaching and the imagination

I wish I could say that what happened to me as a teacher at a university was part of this writer's wild imagination. Instead, I find myself asserting the facts. There is no imagination needed to stake my claims. Everything stated in *Book of the Other* really did happen. Someone might dispute the exactness of my timeline. To that I say, racism happens and then it keeps on happening. Once enacted and embedded, it stays with you like a sliver that gets deep beneath the skin. It festers and reaches into the future. It marks a moment and becomes memory. It is why I am writing about it even now. This essay is supposed to be about teaching. Racism, enacted on me by other teachers, informs my perspective as a teacher. That it will always be within proximity to everything that I write or say or do. In that way, racism could claim victory, because what some white people did in that university, in that department, forever changed me as person. For the life of me, I cannot seem to write about flora and fauna. I write about race as though my life depended on it. I state this as a teacher. This is about teaching, after all.

On the unwanted cadence of memories

At some point in the reading of this book, you might find yourself asking, "Didn't I just read this a few pages back?" Or, "Why does this sound so familiar?" Well, that's because you did just read this; it's happening all over again. It's when the act of writing becomes enacted. This looping of language or images or stories is really the enactment of something that happened. It keeps on happening. I am talking about race. No. I am talking about racism, this looping as a violence that happens on a physical, psychological, and emotional plane. Racism, when it occurs, has a way of extending into the past. Once it's happened, it's always present, always happening. I for one, am tired, holding this burden of anticipating. Wait for it. Wait for it. Does this count as a claim on seeing the future? Is this clairvoyance if one knows the inevitability of racism's arrival? It's just a matter of preparing for the when.

The story of being summoned into a room, of being accused by little white boys for stealing, of being singled out and questioned by the mother of a white boy for her loss of five dollars and a child's loss of dignity, this first happened at the age of 10. Once it happens, it keeps on happening. There is a crime still being committed, the culprit a privileged white male still on the loose. Whiteness runs rampant then and now. This happened in the fourth grade, in 1979, and still this story is being written, again written into the consciousness of this moment and for all the future iterations of wanting to put this memory down. By this time tomorrow, my steps will feel weighted again. I will move forward in this book and the living book that is. At some point in the future, be it a week, or a year, distant or more likely nearer, I will write of what happened yet again. Still in an effort to put it down. Still with the knowledge of this being present.

On Family

On love and cruelty, mother and son

I see my mother twice a year at best. We live 300 miles apart, but we might as well be in different countries on different continents. We exist in different times with different wants, being a mother, a son. I say all this to say, we are more apart than we are together. But however different or distant we have become, she is always looking for ways to be my mother.

When I told her that I was away on a residency, this gave my (at the time) 89-year-old mother ample reason to call obsessively on the hour. She thought that I would be alone, as though I was not already alone. She worried that something would happen while I was away, or so I thought. After the fourth call on this day, of answering and dropping and answering and dropping, I told her that she was no longer allowed to call, as though I were the parent prescribing allowances. There was no reception where I was residing, and I would find a way to call her in the morning, once, and that was all. I said that I was (at the time) 53 years old and she could no longer treat me like a child. To this, my mother said that she was lonely. That was all. She said, "Sorry." She hung up the phone. Why am I compelled to write this and share it?

What you've just read was the first of what I believe will be many attempts. I am revisiting this months after I first wrote these words. I am realizing this time, I'm the one who's lonely. That is all. No one is telling me when and who and the number of times I am allowed or willing to call. There are no issues with reception. Nonetheless, I am alone. I am starting to worry that something will happen.

I am now 57 years of age and not yet treated as someone old. All this time, I have been wrong. My mother is not treating me like a child. She is treating herself as someone old. She wants to know that I am all right. She is also letting me know that she is all right. I want to say I'm sorry to my mother, but a lifetime of apologies amounts to a single and repeating note encompassing sadness, regret, mourning for all the loss and all that is still to be lost.

On all the things we still cannot say

I am going to write this without judgment. This is about people and places far from where I am today. And still, I am hesitant. I am afraid that someone will question its validity, interpretation, or even its reach for the imagination. This is neither fiction nor the truth. It is the piecing together of what I know. Fragments and shards of lives of people I barely knew. I had an aunt, my mother's older sister, back in Vietnam. She was married to a man; from what little I know from stories told, he was not a good man. He married my aunt. They had two boys. He married a second and younger wife because he could, because this was an accepted and legal way of being. This is not a story about the man. I did not know him. I did not once call him my uncle. Shortly after his second marriage, he died of a somewhat mysterious cause. One relative said it was a heart attack. Another said he smoked too much. My mother, when asked, will just change the subject. He died. The end. And this is where my story begins.

My aunt was left a grieving widow with two young boys and a woman she barely knew. What if I told you that they stayed together? They raised the boys together and the boys called them "mothers" and nothing more. They raised the boys to become kindhearted men who married women who gave them children who called my aunt and my other aunt "grandmothers." This would have been enough of a story. What if I told you that the two women took the money that was theirs by marriage? They bought some land. They built a home. They started a business.

The younger of the two women designed and sewed beautiful dresses. The older of the two women discovered her talent for doing business. She sold the dresses and they made a killing. They lived through a war. They lost everything. They stayed together. They rebuilt their business. They rebuilt their home. My aunt lived well past her eighties. She died. Two years later, my other aunt died.

What if I told you that this is really a story about language or better yet the lack of language? I grew up thinking there was no word for who I am in spoken or written Vietnamese. No word for gay or lesbian or trans. When I returned to Vietnam as an adult, I was asked if I was straight or crooked. The man pointed and then gestured with his finger. I laughed along. I was told that gay men were referred to by the initials B.D. It stood for "bong duc." Translated, "bong duc" means the shadow of a man. What if I told you that I saw my *bac* (older auntie) and my *co* (younger auntie) both in their eighties before they died? I heard my cousin say *me* (mother) out loud. I heard both my aunts respond at once, and then they laughed, again in tandem. "Sometimes it's just easier," my aunt said to me. "It's just easier when there is no language to signify, differentiate, complicate, or contain." What if I told you? What if you read this? What if I told this story as a novel? Is this still the truth? Is this just a beginning?

On the fear that comes with being chosen

I am a godfather to a boy born to a Vietnamese mother and a white father. I was connected to this child before he was born. I was his mother's teacher. She found her way into my classroom, a Vietnamese woman writing poetry in English and a Vietnamese man teaching English by writing poetry. To some, this might be a small or minor detail, but to us, this was the glue of a lifelong bond. We are, most of the time, friends, family, constantly present in one another's lives. Countless times we had pho as a family, boba runs, matzo ball soup, and yes, that one time my godson shared his acquisition of language when he said, "Truong, don't be a pussy."

I am connected to my godson as I am connected to his mother. I hosted the baby shower to welcome his arrival. His first birthday was held in my home and the guests, many of whom were Pentecostal Christians, found themselves surrounded by my art, made from the images of naked men. His mother and I did this knowingly and with a sense of pride, perhaps with the hopes of one day telling him this story of how his first birthday party went down. My mother is knitting my godson a sweater. She has never met this stranger of a boy, but still, she believes he is family. I am connected to this child in ways I cannot even begin to express in words. But the fear remains, always the fear of one day hearing from a figure towering over me, "You're nothing like me. I love you. I don't even like you. You are my family. Who are you?" I live with this fear of not knowing how to hold.

On all that is still in between

Because I got no reception at the residency, my 89-year-old mother resorted to texting me in the language of our native tongue. It is a language I do not really read and a source of shame that I, as a 57-year-old man, do not read the language of my mother. And still, I try in all my brokenness to respond, short, to the point, misspelled, and once denounced as petulant. It's not that I am, but my Vietnamese is that of a 10-year-old child rebelling against the added hours of having to attend Saturday Vietnamese language school.

I'm on my laptop bingeing a recommended show, a character study of a Black man separated from his mother at birth. She is no longer alive but as an adult he is finally reunited with her spirit while swimming in a lake in New Orleans. In this peculiarly dramatized scene, the mother says to her grown son, "Me yeu con." Translated into English from the Vietnamese language, the phrase says "I love you" from a mother's perspective. How is it that I am hearing this spoken by the character of a Black woman to her Black son? The story that led me to that scene is sordid and detailed and full of implausible drama that somehow works on screen. Perhaps the real question is, how is it that neither my mother nor I have yet said that phrase, those words, to one another, from either perspective, in any language for that matter?

My 89-year-old mother's love arrives as text messages. It arrives in response to my response in broken Vietnamese. My mother always makes a point of telling me how happy she is, how proud she is, and always she ends with a note that reads, "Cam on con." Translated, it means "Thank you, son." She would text this, again and again. I would receive it, hold it, each time encountering the weight of her words as though I am looking for a way to put them down. Across a country, an ocean, a chasm created by all that is lost in the act of translation, she is still trying to be a mother. And who am I to speak or write these words? At three years past the half-century mark, I am still that child that pushes and pulls at his mother's coat sleeve. "Cam on con," my mother writes.

In that scene in the show, the mother tells her son to let go of his pain, to put down all the things he's been carrying, to release and relinquish. The scene plays out as a surrender. The son lets out a primal scream. The mother whispers, "Me yeu con." The son, played by Sterling K. Brown, says, "I don't know what that means." I was told of this show, of this particular episode, by a student who wanted me to see it for the specifics of that Vietnamese phrase. I watched it, watched the painfully awkward reach of that narrative dramatization, and thought, "If only my mother could watch this show." I thought she would love the melodrama of it all. In case you're wondering, the show is titled *This Is Us*.

On the impossible story, life, and my mother, always my mother

As a six-year-old, I devoured the English language, so much so that I was a child one day, an adult the next. That is to say, I grew up emotionally long before my body caught up. This need to adult was born of necessity. My mother needed a bridge to the English-speaking world. A number of factors may have contributed. I answered the door when strangers knocked. I was the youngest of five siblings; I was around, always around, when no one else could be bothered to answer. I was precocious enough to always speak. Even as a child, I wanted to have my way with words, in particular, those words my mother, at the time, could not gain access to. I was my mother's interpreter, her voice, her witness to all the complications of living in a new and unfamiliar country. I still remember that time in the first grade when my mother came to school to play the role of my mother in a parent/teacher conference. I told my teacher in advance that I would have to be present for my mother. I remember sitting in that room next to her, the strangeness of that moment of being her child, protected, and her translator, her voice, her protector, adulting all at once at the age of six.

Had this been about a six-year-old boy, the memory could end here as one of many memories that shaped me into the man I am today. But this is not the story of a child but that of a mother, who up to this point has been portrayed as helpless for her lack of the English language. My mother sat nervously waiting in the chair. My mother, the teacher, and I all sat waiting. And then appeared a man, a Vietnamese man who spoke both English and Vietnamese, who spoke with the ease of knowing the teacher, of knowing his role as an interpreter. But most surprisingly, he spoke with the ease of knowing my mother. This familiarity was unmistakable. They knew one another from something in the past. She spoke. He listened. He translated. She heard. And I was relegated to the role of child and, once again, witness. But amidst the ease, I could not help but notice a tension.

My mother learned English in the years that followed, as a means of survival. She went on to start her own business, first as a seamstress, then a tailor, then the designer of one-of-a-kind dresses. She saved enough money, along with my father, to put a down payment on a home. She learned to drive. She got a job at a phone factory assembling phones, which later evolved into the work of soldering chips to motherboards. Long after my father's passing, my mother retired at the age of 65. She came home one day with a catalog filled with items that would commemorate her years of working at the company. I think she chose an engraved watch, or was it a crystal vase? I remember having that conversation and harboring a sadness for her happiness at arriving.

Years later still, my mother went on a road trip with my nephew. They drove from LA to San Francisco. He dropped her off at my apartment. She spent the day knitting, praying, and telling stories from a lifetime of clustered, complicated living. She spoke of the time in my first grade when she encountered that man. It was revealed in her retelling that the man was my father's commanding officer. It was also revealed that she knew him from a sordid past, that she had a history of bribing him, paying him the sum of my father's military salary. In return, he kept my father off the front lines of the war. "Your father never knew," my mother said. "He took pride in being a strategist and so I kept it a secret. I just needed to keep him from getting killed." Having surrendered my father's military salary, how then did she feed a family of five in the midst of a war? My mother sold rice and cognac on the Vietnamese black market.

That's a story for another time.

On righting a wrong and retelling a story

I wrote this story once before. I wrote it as a poem from the perspective of a child, curious and perhaps still looking for a hero. The protagonist of that poem was a man, my uncle. I knew he liked to drink red wine. He liked smoking. Other than that, I knew very little about my uncle, except for the stories: romanticized victories of a war that was inevitably lost. I know even less about my aunt, whom I made into an inadvertent antagonist. I am rewriting this story in sentences in the hopes of achieving a certain clarity, of knowing, of finding this woman still inside, somewhere deep inside this story. She married an officer who rushed off to war. She married the stories of his heroism, of the battles won and battles fought, but never was there talk of any killings. She married into a life of waiting, waiting for life, waiting for death, waiting for word, for days and for weeks, waiting. She married into whispers, rumors finding their way home, of his betrayal and of his mistress, and of his love, his love of war, his mistress the war. She married into a seething anger. She listened to stories. She waited for word. One day while waiting as he was still waging war, she placed her hand flat on a table. She slid her ring up. She cleaved her finger with the ring intact. She sent him the finger and the ring in a box with a note. To this day, she still holds a handkerchief in her right hand. She smiles. She laughs. She has a way of veiling the past. As I am the writer of this story, I am inclined to say that this was, this is, a love story. I could be wrong in my observations. They outlasted the war with their marriage intact. They crossed an ocean. They learned a new language. They lived together in relative peace. They never had children. They shared a love for *Gone with the Wind*. He died of old age. She lives alone. She called me the other day and asked if I wanted the commemorative framed plates of Rhett, Scarlett, and Mammy. She says it's a way to remember him, should I choose to remember him.

On the spectacle of my mother saving the family

On April 27, 1975, my mother tore down curtains and quickly sewed backpacks and tote bags, one for each member of the family. She instructed the older children to pack the bags with a change of clothing, toothbrushes, and whatever else could translate into currency. This was the story that I've been told again and again. As the youngest in the family, I was convinced that we were all going on a trip. My father came home that evening from the war. He took off his uniform, his jacket, shirt, pants, socks, and shoes. My mother had a change of clothes waiting for him, a nondescript shirt, pants, and sneakers to convey the invisible living of a civilian. She burned the uniform. As the story goes, he buried the medals deep at the foot of a banyan tree, hoping to return to claim his belongings. We pretended to sleep that evening, but a simple nudge from my mother in the middle of the night was all we needed. My father's best friend drove the entire family to the port. Along the way, we picked up the friend's nephew. If anyone asks, my mother instructed, I was to say that he was my brother.

We arrived in the dark. We sat waiting at the port, with no particular way of getting out. In her version of the story, my mother said that my father wanted to go home. She said he said, "We have each other. We'll be all right." My mother refused. She later retold the story with an addendum to her refusal. She said of that moment, "There was no way I was going to raise you and your brothers and sisters alone." My mother wandered through the chaos of that port. She found a Korean tanker in the midst of evacuating its citizens. I don't know how she got on board or how she found the ship's captain, but she did. She found him and convinced him that she was the sister-in-law of Vietnam's ambassador to Korea. My mother concocted this lie on the fly. She was carrying a clutch, her one possession of value, given to her by the wife of said ambassador. It was gifted to her for having been a guest at dinner, for having a sister, my aunt, who was this woman's secretary. As luck would have it, a picture of this ambassador's wife was tucked inside the little black clutch. My mother lied her way onto this tanker and brought her husband and children plus one, along for the ride.

Not long after the ship departed, my mother's lie was brought to light. The captain wanted to dock on the island of Phu Quoc to expel our family as stowaways. My mother again sprang into action. She sat down on the ship's deck. She wrapped both arms and legs around a pole. She screamed and shouted. She said something to the effect of, "You are leaving us here to die. They are going to kill us." My mother cried. She begged. She deliberately made a spectacle of herself. In doing so, my mother convinced this captain for a second time.

When the Viet Cong forces surrounded the ship and demanded the return of the Vietnamese on board, the Korean captain of this ship held his ground and gave the order for his sailors to prepare to fight. He refused to allow the Viet Cong on board to search. The story, as I've been told it, was that this standoff could have resulted in another war. That moment passed, as did our ship. We arrived on the shores of Busan, South Korea. My aunt, being the secretary to the Vietnamese ambassador, was already there, stranded and without a country. She was watching this arrival on television. In her version of the story, my father was spotted with a child on his back. That was me. My mother was probably busy selling or trading something or another. That was my mother, always doing what needed to be done. That was how she carried our family out of a war, across an ocean, and into this version of our lives.

On writing as a way of saying I'm sorry

My father's story was that of a gardener who wandered his way into a war, out of duty. Perhaps for him, it was the right or only thing to do. He thought the income paid for tuition. He thought it kept his kids in school. My father went to war and was shot in the leg. He kept this bullet nestled inside his body. He said it was a souvenir from a life he never cared to live.

My father tended to my brother's garden, a gift he gave to his oldest son and his son's boyfriend. He planted a tree.

He went to war again one year at Thanksgiving when war arrived, this knife fight of words that happened annually when my mother would exact her will as it related to the family gathering, her precarious existence between her homophobic, war hero brother and a gay son and his boyfriend. On that day, my father said exactly what needed to be said. He said to my mother: if it came down to having to choose, I choose my son over your brother.

◎

My father's story was that of a memory, faded and fated. He was shot, but did he shoot? I want to believe that he never pulled the trigger, ever, in response. I remember that one time when my parents argued. They were both grabbing at something. There was a struggle, and then he let go. My mother fell. My siblings said, "You hit her. You hit her." We accused our father of striking our mother. My mother said she fell. She lost her balance. Without knowing, we struck first. We now live with this burden of knowing we struck first. My father left. He came back the next day. My father, years later, spoke with me about the memory of that day. He said that he could not bear the thought that his children could think that he was capable of hitting her.

⊙

My father's story was that of a foreigner, an exchange student at West Point, in other words, a guest. He shook the hand of the former First Lady, Eleanor Roosevelt. He said, "There is a picture somewhere in some archive of me and this giant of a woman." He made a point of noting, "She's like your mother. She makes all the calls." He came to learn. He was conditioned. He was politely told where he should sit, and where not to sit. "Not there," they said. "That's where the Blacks, the all-colored cadets sit." My father told me this story of being the guest, of being the other that they said was different from the other. He warned me of this, of when they would no longer see us as guests. He said to me, "Guest or not, you choose to sit where you want to sit." On his last day as a guest at West Point Academy, he chose where he wanted to sit. My father conditioned me with this story of the work that was needed for unlearning what's fed, forced, ingrained, and learned.

⊙

My father's story was that of an absent father only because he died too soon. He did nothing wrong, other than the fact that he took an interest in the life I coveted. Was that so wrong? I have no one to blame, so I blamed him for robbing me of my right to make amends, to say I'm sorry for all the things and this one thing. I won my first writing prize in my senior year of college. I called my father with this news, and then I took pleasure in refusing him the right to be proud, to attend the awards ceremony. He wanted to go. He asked my brother to drive him to Berkeley. I told him that I would not be in attendance. I was busy with finals. I went to that ceremony without him knowing. My father died in the summer of that year.

◉

My father's story was that of a writer who never wrote a single story. He never read books. He told stories. He collected scraps of my writings. He kept them in a box beneath his bed. He translated the words he did not know. He wrote it in the margins, in response. "What makes this poetry?" he asked on a page crumpled, discarded. My father reclaimed these words by smoothing, weighting flat this stack of pages. These gestures, this want, I did not know this of my father. My writing was something I kept from him. All those years, I did not know. He kept this secret of keeping, collecting, being in conversation with my words. Thus, this is a poem in a book of stories. My father's story insists on being written in the cadence of poetry. I want to think he had a hand in writing this story, that is, in writing this poem.

On the imagined story of my brother

On my eighth birthday, my brother took me to the soda shop at the strip mall across the street and far from home. This was my perception as an eight-year-old boy. I'd crossed that street several times before but always accompanied by someone older and always with the fear of being hit by oncoming traffic. Being that it was my eighth birthday, perhaps my brother wanted to make a point, to teach me something. He crossed the street ahead of me. He stood on the other side and waved me over. It was always a busy street. There were no stoplights to help us get to where we wanted to belong.

He yelled out taunts and instructions in equal parts. I could tell that he was nervous, but that day my brother was also intent on getting his point across. "Look both ways. Be aware. When you are ready, don't hesitate. Don't be a chicken. No one's going to hold your hand today. You either do it or you don't. Go home if you're afraid. Go home." Having stood there for a good few minutes, I saw an opening and ran as fast as I could through one side of oncoming traffic, a middle divide, and then the other side. I heard a car honk, saw another swerve, and then heard my brother saying, "Are you fucking crazy?" There was something in the way he said those words. I chose to remember them as celebration and admiration of my feat of bravery that day.

My brother had me wait at the wall outside the Alpha Beta. He came back with a stack of comic books. He handed me one. Nothing was said. My brother bought me an ice cream sundae. He sat there watching as I ate. He said, "Slow down. You're making a mess." He said, "Hurry up. I have a game to pitch." That was it. That was the memory of my brother. I suppose something was said somewhere in between that soda shop and our crossing towards home. Somehow, I chose to remember this. What came before and the silence that followed. This silence still.

Why this memory and why this story that's not really much of a story? It's all that I have. It is what remains of this stranger that's my brother. I talk to him maybe twice a year, somewhere in between a cluster of holidays and the occasional check-in when some distant relative, in-law, or friend of a friend needs advice on where to go or what to eat. He lives about 60 miles away but a handful of words keeps us worlds apart.

Well past 50 and still the kid brother, I am still trying to show my worth. I am still looking for that intonation of intimacy and awe. "Are you fucking crazy?" What I would give to hear that question, said in that way, just once more. Just today, my brother called. His wife's aunt's children are sending their children here from France. I offered my place as a crash pad for these strangers. He said he would not impose. He said thank you. He said he will let his wife know of my offer. Then comes the pause, followed by a window of silence, and then this happens, something like this is bound to happen. I am looking for my brother. We last spoke really when I was eight, which would have made him 13. "I'm writing nonfiction now. I'm finally taking your advice." Why did I have to say this out loud? What was I hoping to get in return? "I don't want to belittle what you are doing but you really should think about doing . . ." That was what I got in return, something about Netflix and memories of his childhood neighborhood, and how he was going to tell his story. There is something in the way in which we talk where the sum of my parts is less than the whole.

I started writing this in the morning. I was thinking about my brother today. By coincidence, he called and just like that, the story changes. It becomes the truth. I love my brother, but we are strangers. I love my brother, but do I like him? I love my brother. If you have seen my brother, tell him that I've been looking since the age of eight.

On chicken salad and chicken shit

My version of my brother's story is really not the same story. OK, it's actually my story or exists in proximity to mine, like my memories of my father's memories of war. I am telling it because I am staking a claim. I was always that kid who made shit up. Stories, things, recipes, weapons, and shit, all made up from the debris and detritus of my surroundings. I'm telling this story to settle a dispute. Should my brother ever write his story, he will claim many things, but one thing I vehemently object to is the part where he made weapons and provided them to the other kids in the neighborhood for use as protection. It's a strange detail to dispute but, you see, I was the kid who made up shit and I am still the guy who's making up stuff with words and with objects. I'm a maker of things from found objects. On my best days, I might even call myself an artist. Fuck it, I'm an artist. But that's a detail for another story.

This is about weapons made from old brooms that went missing from my mother's utility corner. These foot-long lengths of wood were cut down from larger broomsticks and mops left unattended from the neighbors' porches and yards and backyards in the night. Two halves joined with six inches of chain, a couple of eyehook screws, and you have a weapon to emulate none other than Bruce Lee himself. Choco sticks or nunchucks, as they were known. For an even more intimidating look, I wrapped the wood in black electrical tape. I'm not sure how many of these things really saw action as weapons in any form of combat. But it was I who made these weapons of self-harm—on more than one occasion, I saw boys whack themselves on the noggin while doing their best imitation of the Dragon entering—and likely of no real destruction.

I made them at first as curiosities and then to enact my obsessions with the genre and then it made sense to make them and sell them, provided the kid who wanted nunchucks would provide me with a broomstick, a mop, or a rake, in addition to the cost of constructing these contrabands. I made a killing selling these weapons, toys, and cultural identities because that's what we were when we were kids, immigrants and others trying to lose our identity as other. If I made these weapons today, I would recontextualize, craft, and hang them in clusters on a wall. Call it art. I get to claim this story because my brother is busy injecting Botox into his clients right about now. Why is it important to claim this story? Because this is the story of my becoming. I make things up. I make things out of the things discarded. This is a story about art after all. As the saying goes. You make of it what you make of it. Chicken salad or chicken shit?

On the Great American Story Becoming a Netflix Miniseries

In my brief conversation with my brother over the phone the other day, he talked of wanting to make a Netflix show about growing up in the neighborhood, a place he lovingly refers to by its nickname: "Xom Rac" ("the garbage neighborhood"). Built on top of a city dump, Xom Rac was ground zero for the hopes and dreams of the newly arrived. How fitting that this dream of America was strewn with garbage, crabgrass, and gangs. My brother wants to tell his story about a place that will take its place as an emerging America in the tradition of *West Side Story* or *Gangs of New York*. Was there ever an American story told and made into a movie about a Vietnamese place, like *Chinatown*? His story I'm sure will inevitably become a heroic one by virtue of being the story of the underdog, the quintessential narrative of struggle and strife and overcoming. In his case, it is the story of a bunch of broken and broke boys who came together as Vietnamese. It is the story of the old saying, last one in is the first one out. Out of luck and out of fucks left to give, a band of Vietnamese boys come together to fight and not only fight but also thrive. My brother's story would lead us to the present, where my brother is now a doctor, a man of community stature who has long since abandoned the stench of Xom Rac. With distance comes this wanting to frame all the discarded details, in the hopes of arriving at something worthy to be told and retold. I am writing this, but this is not my story. Maybe one day this will be published in a book. Maybe it will be read by some authority at Netflix or Disney or Amazon; heck, why not? Maybe they'll come knocking and I will give them my brother's number, if I still have it. Maybe this story will be made into a movie or a show. Maybe tomorrow, I'll wake up to tell my version of this story.

On memories of Saturday afternoons at the Jose Theater

Growing up in the seventies in San Jose was all about territories and turf wars between Vietnamese and Mexicans. We fought at every opportunity, be it in school or at the mall or on the playground, in the parking lot of the Stop and Go, the drive-through at Jack in the Box, and, of course, the dining room at Denny's, always at Denny's. Had we stopped to consider our reasons for fighting, perhaps we would have realized our differences were few and our likenesses many.

We were immigrants. Our families were poor. We lived in the same neighborhoods; our parents spoke and broke language with the intonations of other rhythms, other places, and other homes. We ate many of the same foods and shopped at the same supermarkets, like the Pink Elephant, where beans, rice, and tripe were staples of our mother's cooking. Granted, my mother always found it perplexing that beans would be eaten as a savory dish. At the checkout stand, there was no difference between being Vietnamese or Mexican. We emptied our pockets and purses of food stamps and cash. We gave when asked long before we learned the practice of giving back. That is to say, we were conditioned to know this drill all too well.

Despite the fighting, we also shared a sacred ground. Believe it or not, I'm not talking about church. (I remember skirmishes even at church, at least in the parking lot. I believe that still counts as a fight at church.) I am talking about the Jose Theater, where you always made a point of wearing a jacket and covered-toe shoes and lining your seat with the current edition of the *Mercury News*. Vietnamese and Mexicans, boys and girls, parents and children, all sitting in the same theater watching a band of Chinese heroes banding together to exact revenge.

The villain was always older and wiser, with white hair. These were times when adhering to formula was a comforting way of life. The hero sacrificed himself with an epic and prolonged scene of dying. The bad guy always got his in the end. There was never an exception to this rule. And we as a community, Mexicans and Vietnamese alike, sat in that theater intently watching, reading, and learning from the captions of broken English.

On the broken teapot

When my father passed, I did not cry. I tried to induce tears to the extent of listening to Annie Lennox's version of Cole Porter's "Ev'ry Time We Say Goodbye" on repeat for an entire day. Still, there were no tears. I loved my father. He was my best friend. But I was also cruel. I took great pleasure in parceling out my love. I wouldn't let him attend an awards ceremony for a poetry prize I won only months before his death. But with the prize money, I bought him a teapot with a ceramic fu dog on the lid. I spent my entire winnings on this teapot. I gave it to him the weekend of the ceremony. I remember that look of delight as he opened the box. He loved it. I could tell he loved it. He placed it on a shelf perched on a pedestal. Somehow, I thought that was enough to make up for the cruelty.

I graduated college the same year my father died. He gave me a wallet for graduation. Inside was a check for $500 and a note handwritten on pink printer paper. It was in Vietnamese. I didn't know how to read Vietnamese, so I asked my sister to translate it for me. I don't remember what he said, but I remember thinking I needed to be alone, just in case I needed to cry. I kept that letter in the same wallet for a good number of years. When I lost my wallet—sooner or later it was bound to happen—I panicked, having lost my credit cards, debit card, and ID. I forgot about the letter, as I often do with lots of things. The realization of losing something comes with the reconciliation to having lost it. It's really not that big of a deal, you tell yourself. It's gone but it's just a thing. I lose things all the time. It's actually the months and years and decades later that makes remembering so hard.

I finally cried on the 49th day after my father's passing. This day is part of a mourning cycle and an occasion to gather and laugh and remember. In many ways, it's a party. My niece, who was around four years of age, was trying to help clean when she accidently knocked over the teapot I gave my father. The pot itself miraculously stayed intact. The lid was still usable but the fu dog broke into inconsolable pieces.

Something broke and so I broke. I started sobbing. I blamed myself for not putting it away. I blamed the child, who in turn cried because I was crying. I thought by writing this essay that I was taking a circuitous route to arrive at an apology to a father who kept going, who kept loving even when I was being cruel. Somehow that doesn't feel quite right for this moment in this essay. I will try again, if not in this book, then in my lifetime, again and again. For now, let me say I'm sorry to the little girl, my niece, who grew up to be a loving caring mother in her own right. I'm sorry I made you cry. I'm sorry it broke. I'm sorry I blamed you for my breaking in that moment.

On driving and mourning and loving

This happened in the months that followed my father's passing in 1992. I know this for a fact because my brother and I rarely share any time together, let alone find ourselves in a car together. It is the nature of our family's pact: best to love one another from a distance. We were together because we were still sorting through the knotted mess of losing our father. Our mother was somewhere in the same town but still refusing to come home. Perhaps we were on our way to meet up with her or headed to the hardware store to get something to fix this or that. Something always needed fixing in the days and weeks that followed our father's passing.

My brother was driving when the sharp pitch of a siren startled us from behind. He was being pulled over. He must have been speeding or have run a red light. He was asked for his driver's license and registration. He was asked to step outside, to the side and then to the front of the parked car. From the passenger's seat, I could hear the cop talking, asking who the car belonged to. I could hear the cop's strained pronunciation of my father's name. I could hear my brother's response, his efforts to remain calm, almost docile in answering the cop. I could hear the cop saying something about the passenger not wearing a seat belt. He was talking about me specifically, as I was the one in the passenger's seat. Acting on impulse, I opened the car door. I stepped out and said, "Are you really pulling us over for not wearing a seat belt?" What I remember of that moment was the simultaneity of all these things happening. The cop's finger pointed in my direction, his other hand clasped the handle of his gun, his finger on the trigger, and my brother screamed, "Get back in the car!"

It took some time, being talked at and responding with lots of one-word answers of "yes," "no," and the submission of "Thank you officer," before he was allowed back in the car, before he could get us to where we needed to be. I don't remember if we talked or what was said. I remember the drive, his hands positioned on the steering wheel at ten and two o'clock, his eyes looking forward, wet, defiant, refusing of tears. I remember this encounter with the police, the trigger, my brother yelling, "Get back in the car!" Strange and awkward as it might be, I marked it as a rare occasion when one of us as a sibling expressed our love to the other.

On the Book That Came Before

On punctuation and grammar and the prescriptions of the English language

Because I am not made up of infinite language, because I am tired and I want to move beyond this plane of consciousness, because I have been anticipating, thinking, and now manifesting these thoughts into the work of breathing and existing, I am putting them down, putting them here in the hopes that someone will find a need to pick this up, to read these words for comfort or for anger, to use them as a manual to navigate the trappings and ways of whiteness. These answers are attempts and therefore essays on a life endured. Answers are offered out of context to encompass a reach beyond the self or some singular institution of higher learning. This is about the institution of whiteness and racism.

On the use of the period

My tool for writing *Book of the Other*, one might even call it my weapon of choice, was the use of the period as the single form of punctuation: in excess, deliberation, and abundance. I wanted it to be disruptive, physical, relentless. I wanted to punch my way out of the book and out of this subject with the period. There are moments in the book when the period feels rapid and almost bordering on an enacted violence, and at other times, it feels lazy and tired. This is because the book and the writing became true to my nature. I was tired and exhausted, feeling defeated by the subjectivity of racism. The period held that consciousness for me in those moments in the same way that it enacted my desire to break some shit in other moments.

On the footnote as a book

This constraint came in the editing process. My editor did something that I will always be grateful for. She asked questions, tough questions. She kept on asking "Why?" as a way of saying, "You're still not saying." I knew that at some point I would have to answer that question for myself, even as I resisted the expectations of answering it for the other. There was still something that I did not or could not say. At what point does the decision to not say become the enactment of a lie? I found a way to say what needed to be said in the footnotes of the book. It is the book that is hidden inside the book. It is the book that emerges from the book.

On the performance of otherness

I fear that I am incapable of avoiding the performative. I resist. I go so far as to even declare my resistance to the performative throughout the book. It is as though I am reminding myself that I am not going to perform even as I am standing on that stage.

I have been receiving a lot of notes and messages stating a sense of anticipation and eagerness to read my story, to be touched by it, to receive it. I am grateful for all this support, but I am also wary of the expectations that come with these statements. I want people to be compelled by the work, to be moved, perhaps even moved to action. I want to confront and convict those indicted in the work, even if this kernel of knowledge exists only between myself and the particular presence inside the book that I am talking to in that specific moment. I want some readers to experience the desire to unread the book. I want readers to arrive at knowing that reading this text will always be in proximity to living this text. I want to share in the discomfort between reader and writer, but one thing I know I don't want is this: that my life be experienced as the inadvertent entertainment that comes from reading this book. This makes me think about all the times I've read reviews of books that label the work as heartbreaking, heart-wrenching, or generous; these are the prescriptions and/or expectations we bring to our reading of a text. If we could just shift that perspective ever so slightly, perhaps we could let go of our expectations of the writer, the other? Is this just my take or is this the reality of being Brown? A white writer crafts a novel from the perspective of a serial killer and the work is celebrated for its much-needed social commentary. I am trying to tell the truth about my living. I'm telling my story to the white woman who asked me to tell my story, who then looked at me and said without hesitation, "Truong, that's not what happened." My reality is this. Every response to the question is a performance that is embraced, critiqued, or rejected.

On the experimentation of language as a necessity

I don't consider myself much of an experimental poet. If metaphor is a luxury, then I don't think I can afford the price of admission into experimental poetics. My experimentations with language are born of utilitarian needs. I used the period in excess to reclaim some authority over the English language. I'm really saying, "So what if I did? What's it to you?" I used the period as a blunt instrument, as both hammer and spoon to dig my way out, as a representation of my bloody knuckles, punching my way through the story, out of the book. I wrote *Book of the Other* in the first person, second person, present tense, past tense. Again, this was born of necessity. What happens in *Book of the Other* happened before and is happening even now. When I thought I had reached the end, I found that I had more that I needed to say. I wrote a book inside a book of all the things I still couldn't say until I said it in the footnotes. These experimentations are not my wants for the language but rather my needs. They are not meant to abstract or obscure a path through. My experimental poetics, if I am going to call it that, is a way of storing provisions, a way of digging, scraping, punching, in the hopes of one day breaking through and getting the fuck out.

I thought that was a simple enough statement at the time I wrote it. Yet here I am unpacking again. "To get the fuck out." There is a bit of bravado in making that declaration. Where would I go? What would I do? Who am I at the end of all this? *Book of the Other* exists in a loop. It is the retelling of experiences over and over because it was impossible to detail the experiences or the thinking in a single narrative or single poem. There were books written inside of books, and as such, there will be readings and inquiries inside the act of reading this book. How close have I gotten with *Book of the Other* in terms of getting out? I've written that book, an endeavor that's taken 15 years of not just writing but also living and enduring. I am having these conversations in the open. You should know that your questions help in the process of breaking down the structures that have kept the book walled in. My knuckles are bleeding. I am exhausted. Light is seeping through the cracks. Air is finding its way in.

I dedicated that book to my students. It reads, "for my students past. present. future. that you might choose to do this work. that you might find these words to be of use. of comfort." How close am I at getting out? I think I'm out. I'm breathing. I'm holding the book. Its weight in my hand is weight off my body. In this beginning, I'm still a teacher. Everything else is still in process.

On honesty as a writing constraint

I set out to write *Book of the Other* with the constraint of honesty. This sounds simple enough, but there are all sorts of trappings inside that constraint, especially if you are a person of color writing in the English language. There is an expectation that you will fulfill the work of being a truthsayer. Yet there are also expectations for that truth. It has to be the kind of truth that is desired and prescribed. It's the kind of truth that performs otherness. But if you write a book based on your truths, *the* truth, or even the facts, for that matter, you reverse the gaze and hold that gaze to the ones who are seeing you as the other. If you write a book that says, "I am looking at you," there is the chance your audience will look away, your reception will be one of silence, your presence erased. *Book of the Other* is that book.

When truth is what I am trying to convey, I am preparing myself for the fiction that will likely be constructed as a response. Imagine telling your story to someone who just asked you to tell your story. Imagine being told by this same person that the story you told is not your story, that they have a version of your story that they consider to be the truth. I do not need to imagine this. It has happened and it will happen again. I am a Brown body moving through white spaces. This is to be expected. Truth becomes a matter of perspective. I wrote a book about the facts.

On silence again

There is a culture of fear that is so ingrained into my everyday existence. I was afraid of losing my job. I was afraid of that book. I was afraid that when *Book of the Other* found its way into the world, it would say everything I wanted and needed to say and it would be met with silence, a silence that would force me back into silence. I was afraid my truth, the truth, would be misconstrued. That is to say, every time I do a reading from that book, I am making a conscious decision of what not to read because I am still afraid of what it means to tell the truth. This freedom of expression is something I am always working towards in my writing, but I cannot claim that I've arrived at this consciousness in the book or life.

Working and writing as a person of color in the English language, in this country, my voice is always being silenced. It happened when the white chair of my department politely directed me to refrain from expressing my anger, frustration, or resentment when talking about race because it violates some measurement of professional conduct. It happened when the white male colleague wrote in an interview evaluation, "Truong is nice but small in comparison." It happened when silence was both imposed and chosen as a form of expression. It has taken me 15 years and four publishers to arrive. My right to express freely has been challenged. I wrote that book based on the facts out of concern that someone will challenge the perspective of truth.

On perspective

I didn't know how to prepare for this book. I cleaned my home obsessively. I gave away the many objects I collected over the years in my efforts to hold on to past histories. I threw out materials I hoarded in the hopes of stockpiling ideas for future artistic endeavors. I am sitting in a dark room except for the single bulb that casts enough light to write these sentences. I am trying to be present.

If *Book of the Other* belongs to the reader, the reader should know that I've stated in the book that there is always room next to me, should you choose to walk next to me. If the reader sees themselves inside the book, that the book was written because of and about them, that too is a reality inside the book. It occurred to me, while writing these statements, there is yet another perspective. Some are not standing next to me, nor do they see themselves inside or implicated in the book. They are walking in the same direction as I am walking. They maintain their distance from across the street. They may never cross the street, yet they are seen from my perspective. This is yet another reality.

On courage and bravery

A lot of people have commented on the bravery or courage of that book. I know such comments are conveyed as a way of honoring or caring or supporting the book. With that said, I've learned that I am uncomfortable receiving those accolades. I was writing the truth about what had been happening to me. I was stating the facts in an effort to write myself back into existence. I shouldn't have had to be courageous or perform some act of bravery. Speaking the truth should be no different than breathing or laughing. It should be a part of our daily existence, and yet it is not. It is made to be this feat of human accomplishment, a rarity. As such, it perpetuates the culture of silence and fear that precedes our considerations of truth. I have been writing with this fear and living with this silence for far too long.

I had to ask myself some difficult questions while writing *Book of the Other*. What are you afraid of? At what point does silence become the lie you live with? The book is an answer to those questions. It is the breaking of silence.

On policing grammar

The difficulties have resulted in so many iterations of *Book of the Other*. The book in its current form is a culmination of years of writing, living, and enduring. At one point, this book was punctuated by a cis-identified white male. He is a friend. I asked him to police the grammar of this book. It occurred to me that the act of policing is so present in our relationships to language and each other. I wanted to enact that police state in my work, to enact that lack of authority in my writing, to enact the conditions of existing as a person of color writing in the English language, in the United States.

The process led me back to my relationship with grammar and language. Why have I been so incapable of claiming authority over this language? Because I am Brown? Because I am dyslexic? Because I am an immigrant? Because I am always reminded of my place when I am told that my English is good, that I speak English with no trace of an accent? I used to say that I write in a borrowed language so that I wouldn't be held accountable. But I am always held accountable for stealing some white woman's crummy five dollars. I didn't take the money, but still, my mother paid her in full.

English is my second language. I only write in the English language. Borrowed or not, I'm not giving it back. At some point in the process of writing and rewriting that book, I decided to do the work of punctuating myself. I chose to mark the entirety of that book with the single action of asserting the period. It felt violent at times. I was using the period as a disruptor. I was using it as a drum-beat. I was using it as a blunt instrument to dig, to spoon, to punch my way out of this subject and *Book of the Other*.

On the uncomfortable truth

I've sat with the discomfort of this subject for most of my life: the discomfort of being othered and accused of taking five dollars from some white woman's purse, that becomes the discomfort of being rejected for a chance to compete for a fair and equitable livelihood, that becomes the discomfort of seeing someone who looks like my mother on the news: she was punched in the face for being an elderly Asian woman.

I've confronted this discomfort throughout my life, in my writing. I live with this discomfort. Once this happens, it never stops happening because I'll always carry the memory of it happening. I move with it through the world. I've learned to share this burden with my community. I put it in the book. I am asking the reader to sit with me, to share in the discomfort and share in the knowing. And just when I least expect it to happen, I am hit with this discomfort yet again.

Today, I received a note from someone I consider to be a friend. They said that they were moved by what's been written about the book, that they were there at the scene of the crime. Wait, hold up. You were at the scene of the crime and you said nothing? That they were looking forward to reading, holding the book. And just like that, the words of a friend could still amount to a gut check/gut punch. Why? And why didn't you say? Why didn't you ask? I want the book to be read, so that the reader might want to unread this book. I want my voice to be heard loud and clear. I want this story to be seen as the truth. And if there is still doubt, I want you to know I've presented the facts.

I want to compel the reader of the book. I want to confront. I want to convict. I want to sit with the discomfort of knowing that someone was present at the scene of the crime, and still it happened. I want to sit with the discomfort of knowing that this book is my life. It happened and perhaps it is happening even now. What I don't want is this: that the book be read as *riveting*.

On letting go

It occurred to me that the act of cleaning my house was very much like the writing of this book. I wanted to let go of my past. I gave away a ton of shit one weekend, bags upon bags of the things I've collected over the decades. I threw out materials and frames all accumulated over the years in the hopes of turning them into art projects at some point in the future. Somewhere in this process over the weekend, I found myself sitting in my home, cleaned, cleared out, decluttered, with everything in its rightful place. I was present in the moment. I wasn't stuck in the past nor was I hoping for a future project or a future life. I lifted the shades in my living room and I found myself sitting in the light and the dark as the day moved through me. All this to say that I wrote *Book of the Other* from a place of truth, facts about what happened to a Brown body in the space of the academy and the truth about my existence in that place. Sometimes telling the truth meant that I had to acknowledge that I was living a lie. I was willing to live that lie to hold on to my place as a teacher in that space. I wrote the book in the same way that I cleaned my house. I put things down. I threw things away. I saw things for what they were. And I saw myself for the first time in a long time. I am looking neither back nor forward. I am dwelling in the present.

On silence

I have been trying to unpack all that's been crammed into this word from years of living, learning, and writing. I am discovering that I've buried so many of my complications inside the word, so much remains unresolved. My first class in grad school was titled The Work of Silence. I used to think that silence was power, a practice of writing that, when invoked, worked as protest. Silence as the absence of language was a way of withholding. This was my consideration of power as a writer, a gay man, a Brown man.

And then it happened. It keeps on happening. This rejection, this denial of a right to a fair and equitable existence. This denial of safety for something as simple as walking down the street, this fear of saying what is true. I'm just going to say it. I worked in that place as an adjunct. I applied for the position of tenure-track professor in this same place time and again. I was denied, rejected, disqualified. It kept on happening, and I was forced to live with the reality that each time I was rejected, a white person was hired. Because I continued working in this place as a lecturer, because I loved my work as a teacher and that rush of connection I got with my students, because I feared that what little I had in terms of a livelihood could still be taken from me, I accepted the transference of shame from the inflictor to the inflicted. I inherited the silence of this happening to me.

Before arriving at what I considered the end of *Book of the Other*, I had to ask myself some difficult questions. At what point did silence become my sin? I taught my students the craft of writing, to own their voices, to be empowered through the work of writing, the work of silence in writing as an act of protest, of withholding. The enactment of silence as an assertion of power. What then was the work of silencing that was happening to me? I remained silent even as I taught the work of silence. I was living a lie. Why?

I wish I could speak to you now about silence as a choice or perhaps an assertion. I like that idea and I continue to hold on to that possibility. To speak of silence in the wake of *Book of the Other* is to speak about the breaking of silence even if there is no language when the silence is broken. Trusting is about meeting that kind of silence and discomfort. I'm talking about the silence that exists in a space, in the academy. I've encountered these moments in my classroom, often when someone writes something difficult, pertaining to race. In recent years, I've been telling my students to sit with the discomfort of what was written, said. Insist on that pause of recognition. Presence in the face of silence. Not all feedback arrives as words or voices. I am trying to do the thing that I teach. I am trying to meet the silence and discomfort with my presence. Even if I am without words, I hope my presence is breaking the silence.

On standing alongside

(FOR SARETTA MORGAN)

What does it mean to stand alongside? I believe that at some point in our paths, be it our careers, artistic practices, or lifetimes, whiteness will encroach. Whiteness will ask that we sign on to the agenda of whiteness. It will ask that we look away, to be complicit with our silence, to let whiteness speak on our behalf. Whiteness might even ask that we champion whiteness, to speak up and say racism did not happen here because I am here within the space. It did not happen to me and therefore I am proof that racism did not happen. Whiteness will ask this of us, and how we choose to answer that call will determine what it means to stand alongside. This all happened to me. Whiteness did this to me. It enacted its racism and discrimination on me and then it asked that I remain silent. I did just that for so many years. I thought I was protecting myself. I thought that being silent kept me within proximity to the work that I do as a teacher and a person of color in the academy. My silence was a contribution to whiteness and was damaging not only to me but to all of us who are trying to create a fair and equitable life for ourselves as Brown and Black people in the academy. It's taken a long time, but I am now 57 years old. I have no real interest in a career. I still want to teach, but that is not a career. It is a way of life. I am a teacher and a writer and an artist and I am someone who believes that I will stand up and stand alongside when it matters. I hope that I have the conviction to reject the expectations of whiteness.

The silence I recently fell back into came from the backlash of having written *Book of the Other*. Whiteness came for me by way of coming after those who supported my work. My publisher and those who spoke openly in support of my book found themselves on the receiving end of another's outrage. Those who came for me also sought out the support and endorsement of another person of color. I have to admit this came as a surprise. I anticipated much in writing the book and putting it out into the world. I thought I was prepared, but I was not. How do you prepare for accusations of misogyny and misogynoir, not for the things you wrote or said, but for the decision of not writing or saying? I chose not to name people inside that book. I chose not to involve Brown and Black people in it, a decision made out of care and deliberate consideration of what inclusion means. The work of *Book of the Other* is not about inclusion. It is about implications. Those who see themselves in the book, see themselves because they have been implicated in the agenda of whiteness. How then do I respond to such accusations of misogyny and misogynoir from someone I thought I cared for? I could engage in this debate but that would mean the spectacle of a conflict between Black and Brown individuals. I am always open to discourse, but I will not respond to the backchanneling of issues as important as race and representation. These are the workings of whiteness, this division. This would be the antithesis of being alongside.

I've been in and out of silence throughout my life. It occurred to me today that I've been waiting all this time for someone to come forth and say that they are willing to stand alongside. I could not ask this of anyone, but I hoped and I anticipated. And then you said it, just like that. You said it in such a clear and matter-of-fact way. "I'm beside you while you voice your pain." It feels like a path through, an arrival. I promise this in return. I will stand alongside you as you navigate through this world of the academy and art and writing. And if such language is needed at that moment, in this lifetime, I will invoke the same language that was said to me out of care, and I will say, "Those motherfuckers." I do not wish my fate on you or anyone, but I am prone to anticipate the workings of whiteness.

I wrote *Book of the Other* for that very reason. When I first started talking about the book, I said that it was about my experiences and that I wanted to say what needed to be said. I think my position and thinking on this subject have changed over time. I no longer think this book was written for me. I wrote the book as documentation. I wrote this book to state the facts. I wrote it to bring attention to the fact that racism, discrimination, whiteness, and its workings are alive and well, thriving even. I wrote it to be thick and heavy in the hopes that this weight will be added to the weight of all that came before, when whiteness enacted its agenda on our Black and Brown bodies. I hope this weight is registered, added to all the weight we have all been carrying all these years. I hope this weight, these facts, become irrefutable. I hope that this weight comes crashing down and lays to waste the agenda of whiteness. This is my hope. This is my belief in what it means to stand alongside. When this all started, I did not know how I would arrive. I did not know this about the book and I did not know you. And here I am writing this sentence that is an arrival. I believe I wrote the book for you.

On history and the imagination

This is not as much an essay as it is a claiming. I woke up this morning with a purpose. I am going to excavate every memory in an attempt to tell the stories tucked into the body. They have been kept there, waiting for this day and the days to come. But first they have to be located in the body. This is not as easy as it seems. Some of these memories are deep inside. They remain because I've tried on more than one occasion to throw them out, along with the anger and pride and resentment and shame that comes with being. Each failing resulted in the memories being placed deeper inside this labyrinth of my body. It is as if I can see myself conducting triage of my own life, my hand reaching into the layers of skin, muscle, and fat to first locate, then dislodge, and then reassemble the fragments and shards.

I believe that my living means I am constantly breaking apart. There are pieces of me that have been lost, that I've hidden away from myself, deep within. I've kept them hidden to the extent that I did not know that I had fragments and shards that needed to be found. I saw myself as a book with some of the pages torn out. There was no plot and therefore no need to move in a line. As such, I committed myself to the preoccupation of fighting for what I was desperately holding on to: dignity, worth, a sense of self.

At first, the story of my mother's heroism across continents, war, and an ocean does not seem to have a clear throughline that would connect it with the narrative of my adolescent awakening of sexuality, or my two aunts who thrived in a world that lacked the language to honor their love, imagined or not, or my unpacking a lifetime's worth of hiding, coping, realizing that my dyslexia is as much *a* way as it is in the way.

This book is everything that *Book of the Other* is not. I am calling this book a work of nonfiction committed to the premise of searching, excavating, and reclaiming memories. I am asserting the imagination where memories fail. Of what is not known, I will rely on the imagination to get me there. Is this allowed? And why am I still asking for permission?

These memories and this imagination are disparate when placed in proximity to another. Perhaps there is no throughline, but I did find a length of twine, coarse, resilient, and strong enough to do the labor of binding the complicated parts that make for the incongruences of something real, my life. These broken parts, when gathered and pieced back together, are not the jigsaw pieces I want them to be. They come back to me as jagged shards, forming images that are held together with this chord of insistence on the imagination.

Acknowledgments

This book exists because of the people who have challenged me and stayed. I am still here because of them, because of you.

To my family, and especially my brother, Thang, who brought me back from the brink of death; this is no hyperbole. And to my nephews, Alex and Tristan, your curiosity and zeal for life give me hope.

To Shawn, your visit and the worry you showed jolted me back into living.

To Chantal and Jennifer, for your presence and care in the early stages of this work.

To my colleagues—Kim, Brinda, Juliana, Stephanie, Tom, Kathryn, Kelli, Christa, Elmaz, Patricia, Susan, and Hayes—thank you. I am grateful to call you colleagues.

To my editor, Garrett Caples, thank you for your patience, your vision, and for staying with the complications of my messy rendering. You understood what this book could be, even when I could not fully see it myself.

To Carolyn, for your generosity and love in helping design the cover of this book, and to Tai, my godson: I hope you find your way to these words somewhere in the distant future.

To my childhood friends—Jenny, Christine, Tri, Huong, Quyen, Diep, Minh, and the gang—thank you for reminding me that life, in all its challenges, heartbreaks, and celebrations, is worth it when you have those who will "ride or die" with you.

To Josh and Kirsten, for staying true to the mantra: "we got us."

To the community at City Lights, thank you for giving me this once-in-a-lifetime opportunity. There was a time when I could not have imagined finding my way here.

To Michael—perhaps the most unlikely of characters, but now a lifelong friend—thank you for your annual visits.

To Jennifer, Maria, Choppy, Griffin, Mimi, and the rest of this motley crew I know as my community, I fucking love you all.

To Damon, always Damon.

To poetry, thank you. I love you. I hate you. You will always be present. You will always be a thorn.

This book is as much yours as it is mine.

About the Author

PHOTOGRAPH BY MARK SU

Truong Tran is a writer and visual artist based in San Francisco. He is the author of numerous books, including *The Book of the Other*, which received the American Book Award and the CLMP Firecracker Prize. His work engages questions of memory, movement, silences, and dislocation, often at the point where language begins to fail. Working across text and image, his practice returns to the tensions between what can be said and what remains unspeakable. He teaches creative writing and art at Northeastern University's Oakland campus at Mills College and continues to make work across disciplines.